Reading and Spelling Through Sound

By Jenny Lamond, with Paul R. Whiting, PhD.

PUBLISHED BY

First published by the Evelyn McCloughan Children's Centre, University of Sydney, New South Wales, 1998, Australia.
ISBN 1-86451-055-2

Copyright © P.R. Whiting & J.M. Lamond, June 1992.

Second edition completely revised and reset, 1998.

Third Edition revised and updated published, 2018

Heart Space Publications, PO Box 1085, Daylesford, Victoria, 3460, Australia.
Tel +61 450260348

www.heartspacepublications.com
pat@heartspacepublications.com

All rights reserved under international copyright conventions. No part of this book may be reproduced, stored in a retrieval system, or transmitted in any form or by any means electronic, mechanical, photocopying, recorded or otherwise without written permission from Heartspace Publications. However, relevant illustrations and charts only may be reproduced on a personal needs basis as a tool for teaching a student to read and spell by the method prescribed in this handbook.

Whilst every care has been taken to check the accuracy of the information in this book, the publisher cannot be held responsible for any errors, omissions or originality.

ISBN: 978-0-9944028-3-7

Table of Contents

Acknowledgements	V
Section 1	**1**
Discovering Reading and Spelling through Sounds	1
Overview	2
Summary of Outcomes	5
The Importance of Intervention	6
Identifying Different Kinds of Reading Difficulty	6
Part 1 Exploring Letter/Sound Connections	**13**
Activity Plan	14
Activity 1: Preliminary Work With Younger Children	16
Common Confusions	16
I have learned about	18
Key Elements for Teacher to Consider	19
Activity 2: Discovering Consonant and Vowel Sounds	20
a. The Consonants	20
b. The 'Safe' Vowel Sounds	23
General Principles	23
Using the Safe Vowel Chart	24
Part 2 Decoding Words	**25**
Activity 3: Introduction to the Decoding Book	26
Listening – One Sound? Two Sounds?	26
TUTOR'S WORD LISTS	29
Activity 4: Talk to your Pencil	30
Activity 5: Safe and Danger Vowels and Bossy (Emergency) 'E'	32
Safe & Danger Chart	34
Activity 6: Ending Sounds /e/ or /i/	36
Activity 7: Double Letters and Swimming Pools	39
Exceptions	42
Activity 8: When Cat 'C' Changes His Sound	43
Activity 8.b: 'c' or 'k' to Start a Word	47
Activity 9: /C/ or /K/ to Finish a Word	49
Activity 10: K Needs One [consonant] Friend Only	53
Activity 11: C Needs One Friend Only	56
Activity 11b: Can C Finish Alone	58
Activity 12: When G Changes its Sound	60
Part 3 Discovering Reading Success (putting it all together)	**63**
Discovering Reading Success	64
Using the Eye-Movement Trainer to Push	69

Part 4 Building Spelling Cleverness — **72**

Word Structure and Finding Links — 73
Word Categories for Studying Spelling Lists — 73
Clues For Catchy Words — 74

Section 2 — 79

Index to the Sound Dictionary — 81
The Sound Dictionary: Building Word Families — 82
Spelling — 84
A Spelling list — 86
Detective Pages in the Sound Dictionary — 89
Detective Steps — 91
Suggestions for Work — 92
Jenny's Sound Dictionary — 94
Phonetic Symbols Used — 95

Appendices — 149

Appendix 1 Writing Revision — 150
Appendix 2 Using the Recorder in Remedial Tutoring — 155
Appendix 3 Adaptations for Whole Class Work — 156
Appendix 4 Additional Words for Seniors — 158
Appendix 5 Illustrations for Processing Words — 162
Appendix 6 Activity Plan and Activity Templates — 164

Index — 174

Foreword

I first came across the work of Jenny Lamond in 1974 when I attended one of her training sessions in remedial reading for teachers. I went reluctantly, not wishing to reject out of hand a method which I assumed would be old fashioned or eccentric. Eccentric it was: eccentric enough to fascinate children and the adults who were learning how to do it. I thought parts of it were silly. So did the children, and they were delighted. It was so different from every approach they had experienced, and yet it did all the important things.

It recognised that it was not the child's fault that they failed. It recognised that most children and adults who fail to learn to read, do so because they cannot easily manipulate the sound symbol system of the English language, with all its complexities. It recognised the importance of multi-sensory approaches in teaching reading to these children. And it recognised that the only motivation that counts in the end is what the educators call "intrinsic motivation" - motivation that comes from success in doing the task itself.

Those are good principles. Jenny Lamond's method is also based on a painstaking analysis of the structure of words in English. This is something that children with problems in reading and spelling have found chaotic and incomprehensible. Jenny's method is able to introduce children to the English written language as a system which can be understood. Understanding leads to confidence and, ultimately, to competence.

There are those who will reject the method because it appears to be mechanical, and to teach skills out of context. To those people, we should say that the most important context is that of the life experience of the child or adult who is seeking help. That is the context that should first be considered. And for most of these people, their experience of reading is of an activity which is to be avoided at all costs. It is stressful and unrewarding in the extreme. To urge therefore, that reading itself will provide the best context for remediation is nonsense. That is why Jenny's method starts with listening and writing, not reading. Only when the child has regained some of the lost self-esteem and confidence in hand written English is reading in context introduced. That is another reason the method is so successful.

Finally, the method is flexible. It is adapted to the needs of the individual student, and can be used either as a total reading and spelling program, or as an element in the broader program. It has been used successfully now for nearly thirty years in individual teaching, small groups and even with whole classes of children. The result is children and adults who feel that they understand how the English or orthographic system works. They are willing to "have a go", are experienced in checking their own work, used to recording what they have learned, and confident about looking up anything that they are unsure about. Most teachers would be delighted to have a class of children with these "process" skills.

But like every other successful method, it will be largely dependent on the teacher. Jenny Lamond believes in children. She assumes that they are capable of succeeding, and she communicates that confidence to them. She knows the disabilities can be overcome, and she teaches that through her approach. The effect of such an attitude on self-esteem is obvious. In the hands of a committed, enthusiastic teacher who also believes that all children can succeed, this method will work as I have seen it work over the years.

Paul Whiting PhD, Faculty of Education, University of Sydney, 2017

Acknowledgements

March 2017

For this third edition of Discovering Reading and Spelling Through Sounds, I heartily thank Dr Paul Whiting, and Peter Lamond for their enthusiasm and support.

This third edition does not change the teaching methods or the ethos of Jenny's original work. However, as many years have passed since the original manuscript was put together, we have modernised it. Many of the sketches have been updated, and of course the layout makes use of current technology.

Pamela Johnson [who has been teaching with the method for over 20 years] and Jenny's niece and past student [who completed the program, as Jenny's student, in 1968] have both offered wonderful support in re growing Jenny's work. To you both, thank you so much, there will be many who will derive benefit from your effort.

Lastly, I would like to acknowledge my mother's (Enid Deal) contribution to Jenny's methods with forty-five years of dedicated work.

February 2017

The original title of this book was Discovering Reading through Sounds, but for this version we have called it Discovering Reading and Spelling through Sounds.

In 1977 Jenny Lamond developed and published 'A Sound Directory' in collaboration with Dr Paul Whiting. This book listed word families arranged according to sounds and spellings, for use in remedial reading programs with primary, secondary and adult pupils. A second edition was published in 1979. Reprinted versions with alterations were printed in 1981, 1985, 1989.

NB: The original Sound Dictionary has been incorporated as Section 2 of this publication and has been renamed 'Jenny's Sound Dictionary'.

In 1992, the first edition of *Discovering Reading Through Sounds* was published by the University of Sydney, New South Wales, under the authority of Dr Paul R. Whiting who was, at the time, in charge of the Dyslexic Children's Centre unit at the university. Over the years the book has provided teachers with a reliable method of intervention that has served to help hundreds of children with remedial needs to overcome their problems and to learn to read and spell with accuracy.

Jenny Lamond was awarded the Order of Australia medal for service to remedial education, particularly through the development of the Jenny Lamond Method of learning spelling and reading.

Introduction

Perhaps the best way to help you, the reader, comprehend the ideas in this program is to take you back with me – back to the problems of a child in a boarding school in remote North China in the 1920s, never commended for continually having top marks in maths, always in trouble for the lack of success at anything to do with letters and words, therefore a failure! Yes, I the author of this program was that child and all I wanted was to understand, so that I could remember by knowing how to "work it out" and become successful.

This was to influence my approach later in programming for children. Understanding from the very beginning has to be paramount for some children, so success will depend on each progressive step being logical, truly from the known to the unknown all the time.

Now, a brief outline of how this program came into being. My dad was on the staff of the Moukden Medical College in Manchuria and my mum was a teacher. After China schooldays, came Edinburgh Scotland, where six years training prepared me for a future career in teaching. There my choice was to return to China, after conquering the fascinating language, I was well qualified for work with children or the elderly and was appointed to take charge of the home school for blind girls and women. Shortly after, along with all the other young workers there, I was ordered out of Manchuria by the Japanese in their takeover (Second World War). Choosing to retreat to Sydney, Australia in wartime was wise and safe, but my next decision was most unwise and incredibly dangerous. After much trauma, I found myself in dire straits in a prison in Fukushima, Japan…

That was the start of my future, not the end of it. By 1944 three children, who could remember no other existence, reached school age. On starvation rations and with no energy even to think, and no materials, I evaded the issue at first but later decide to meet the challenge to teach the children. Using toilet paper (for exercise books) and stolen pencils we set off on an exciting venture. Those three children could read, write and handle number work by 15-8-1945. Little did I guess that I would fall back on their program after the war.

In the 1950s in Roseville, New South Wales, my sister-in-law Mary Lamond, a retired teacher of renown, was approached by the Department of Education in Sydney and asked to investigate the high I.Q. students who were failing in reading and spelling. I was co-opted into this program at the very start by the department. At that time there were no answers.

My discoveries were to come from my own experience of failure as a child, remembering where and why I failed, and from my knowledge of trends in education during training in Edinburgh in the 1930's when the "sentence method" and "sight reading" were being introduced, and from my work with the children in Japan, having to teach without any equipment; I saw these failures now in the 1950's as coming directly from the changes being put in place in the 1930's and at that time decided to stay with the methods used in the classroom so successfully when I was experiencing "pupil teaching" before training. The children then understood what they were doing and were happy to learn.

Roseville in the 50's, in our home, was where the Sydney Remedial Group of Teachers was based and developed. The incoming teachers were delighted to learn and use the program I was in the process of creating because it was enjoyable, quick and successful. The group existed for forty years using this program.

Now for today: still with the children and adults experiencing failure, they are failing to understand from the beginning of their schooling that letters have to be interpreted and not just to be looked at. I misunderstood and most of my students did too.

Being totally unaware of the need to listen carefully in interpreting what I saw written was a problem. "b" sounded the same as /be/ and I did not know any different. What did it matter anyway? Utter confusion. It is the same with the children today. Both "b" and "be" made sounds. SOUNDing it out is useless and open to misunderstanding, or at least most confusing. Let us teach them what the letter "says" first and have them understanding how to read simple text. There is time enough for the alphabet later.

Our responsibility as teachers of these students trying to cope when they do not know what we are talking about, has to be taken seriously. How fast can we remove as crippling a burden as lack of understanding of the child or student who is fast developing a guilt complex? Remediation has to go back to where the confusion started – the beginning of formal education. How quickly can this be done? How much fun, nonsense, how many games or puzzles to motivation them? Where does visual aid support, fast recall of suitable and challenging material demand thinking through and understanding why? In the more difficult spots in their school work, and even falling back on fun and nonsense ways, let them understand the pitfalls in just looking at the e's, y's, k's or c's and only seeing letters. SUCCESS is what anybody wants and is something students of the Lamond method must and can have. They must never be wrong in remediation even if we take the blame. Disillusioned children or students have to see results for their efforts straightaway and these must come without much effort, and logically. I know for I have had them in my care for about forty years and have been one of them. We can no longer say LOOK, LEARN, REMEMBER. That's over, for most of them cannot. Just think of the hundreds of non-readers in the world! Why?

The program has activities for every session that ensure concentration and possible correct answers for the problems presented. In Kyogle, New South Wales, Damien (year five) said, "This makes sense. I can understand". Like most others his progress was fast.

LISTENING skills are developed. The nonsense or fun you hear is easy to remember. Remedial sessions and activities with hearing, thinking and writing have to come before what has been an unreliable and difficult visual approach in trying to read without any basic knowledge or understanding of the behaviour of letters and the effect neighbouring letters have on each other. Quick fingers are a real aid, when visual conceptions are not accurate or reliable. Workbooks become decoding books (where the student cracks the code) so memory is not challenged in these progressive sessions and the student has a useful tool, for here they learn how to search for and define information, be it new or something learned earlier. These challenging exercises or games are most acceptable to the young achievers, and unknown to them the much hated reading is being given a good foundation and yet no book has been presented to frighten them. That is what we promise "no reading" at the beginning. Wait until you know how.

JENNY M. LAMOND, O.A.M

Although the above was written in back when the original method was first published, nothing has changed in as much as children with remedial needs require special attention to help them discover basic letter/sound relationships before they start to learn the alphabet or to read. Certainly they need to understand these before they start to spell.

Profile of Publisher Mr P Grayson
A brief insight as to how this book came to be reviewed and published by this company

I am dyslexic, but when I started school in about 1959, I was considered dumb; sadly I believed them. Needless to say, school was painful and resulted in my leaving, literally on the very legal date to become a bricklayer.

When my mother saw the same issues in my younger brother (seven years younger) she knew something was not right and so set about finding out if there were some teachings that would identify our issues and help. Of course, in those days there was no Internet and so libraries were where most information was gained. After a time she discovered and met Jenny Lamond, who had developed a method of teaching dyslexic children to read and spell. Anyway, Mum went through Jenny's course for teachers. Some forty-five years later Mum, who is now ninety-two, is still just as excited and dedicated to teaching the Jenny Lamond method as before.

But at ninety-two it was becoming too much for Mum and so she tendered her resignation to the principal at the school where she was teaching as a part time remedial teacher. The headmaster was devastated at the thought of Mum retiring, saying that her success is so great with these kids in need, and that no one else knows the Jenny Lamond method. She begged Mom to continue, and she does.

At the time of Mum going through Jenny's teachings she wanted to help me. However, I was far too sensitive and embarrassed, not to mention angry as a result of my disadvantage, for surely being dyslexic is a disadvantage. But Mum always raved about the methods and there was always a litany of stories about yet another child who was now fixed of spelling and reading difficulties.

Sorry, this is long... …anyway, when visiting Mum in 2014 I told her of a project that I want to put into practice, which was to teach indigenous teenagers in rural areas creative writing.

After hearing my intention, Mum, once again but with firmness said, "Patrick" (Patrick was always used when she was being stern with me), "you must take this" (getting out her notes from Jenny, which were all hand written and very dog-eared) "and use it in your work – it must continue!" This time I really listened, and so I Googled and researched, and learnt that Jenny, in conjunction with Paul Whiting, had produced the book. But further research showed that the book was out of print. Being a publisher, who had the learning and emotional issues associated with dyslexia, I knew I had to get this work out to help as many people as possible.

More research gave me Dr Whiting's details, so I sent him an email introducing myself, spoke about Mum's teachings and said that I would like to meet him with the idea of our company publishing the book. The meeting went well, and Dr Whiting was delighted that the work would continue. By this time Jenny has been long since gone, and so I wanted to contact Jenny's family. They were also keen for the work to continue, and like Dr Whiting, they are keen to support the process. So I received the original manuscript and numerous newspaper cuttings, interviews and the like. But more importantly, I received contacts, both from children who had been taught, and teachers of the method. All, have wonderful testimonies as to the value of the Jenny Lamond Method.

I have decided, with the permission and of Jenny's family, and Dr Whiting to form a Jenny Lamond Foundation, with the idea of propagating the work. Teacher training accreditation and certification program are about to commence.

Pat Grayson, CEO, Heartspace Publications

Section 1

Discovering Reading and Spelling through Sounds

Overview

This book is intended for parents, teachers, and anyone else who wishes to help children or adults that struggle with reading and spelling. It is a practical handbook, setting out in detail a method of applying theoretically sound principles of reading remediation to the needs and abilities of students. Anyone who has a love for children, a desire to help them, and a sensitivity to their responses can use it. And teachers/mentors that have the opportunity to help youth and adults remedy a weakness in the areas of reading, spelling and writing can use it.

The method helps poor readers and spellers discover what they do not understand about written language. Research has shown that deficiencies in comprehension can often be traced to difficulties with processing print itself. A remedial program must begin by replacing faulty habits of hearing and seeing words with reliable ones. Only then can reading be successful.

This method began as an attempt to face the problems typical of remedial situations. Jenny Lamond recalls how it began:

"When I think of David, the first little boy I helped, I am just so ashamed. He was to come for reading, so we read. Well, he just couldn't read. And we read – and he couldn't read! Well, how crazy could you be? I tried for a couple of days and then thought, 'This is

> **How to avoid saying "No! you're wrong!" The Importance of Consistent Positive Reinforcement**
>
> **Example from Part 2 - TALK TO THE PENCIL -** Have a chart of the processing words diagrams in sight. (see photocopiable chart appendix 5). Below are some possible positive reinforcement responses to use when the student is uncertain, or makes an incorrect response. The aim is to allot "blame" away from the student, and to encourage a reasoning method of approaching the task.
>
> **a. When about to write:**
> 1. Which pathway on the chart will you take?
> 2. Be sure to connect up before you start.
>
> **b. After a partically successful attempt:**
> 1. Check (on chart). Which pathway did you use?
> 2. Which picture shows the way your word went?
> 3. Ask, "Is that right? (I didn't say you were wrong!)"
> 4. Did you have a reason for writing that?
> 5. What did your ears hear me say?
> 6. Sorry, I didn't say that word properly!... Let's try again (word repeated clearly by teacher).
> 7. What did I say? Sorry, I'll try again.
> 8. Are you ears and fingers ready to check?
>
> **c. After Self-correcting (usually with a "clue"):**
> 9. That's good detective work. Are you ready to try again?
> 10. Good, you fixed it. Put the tick your self.

mad; I'm making him feel worse instead of better; he's got to feel better!' So I realised that I was at the wrong end of the whole thing."

So what is the answer? How can we take the pressure off the learner and still develop the language experiences necessary for reading competence? Perhaps by helping the student to synthesise words by listening to their sounds. This means working through spelling. Poor readers are also poor spellers. Spelling ability and reading ability are closely related. While it is true that a fairly good reader may also be a poor speller, a poor reader is always a poor speller. It follows that if we teach a person to spell, their reading ability will almost certainly improve. At the simplest level, once the difference between alphabet names of letters and the sounds made by these letters has been made clear to students, it is possible, with some training, to write any English word that is approximately phonetically regular.

Throughout this program, two principles are paramount, namely:

1. <u>The student must be right</u> (for nothing succeeds like success itself). The teacher or remedial teacher starts by recognising that the student needs a warm and pleasant environment, one which makes no demands, but encourages the student to talk and act and feel confident once again, and to grow from success to success. The relationship must be one of complete trust and without any fear (of judgment or impatience) so that the student may open to learning as a bud unfolds to the sun in spring. In the remedial situation, the student is always right. If the learner hasn't learned, the teacher hasn't taught. (See the box: "How to avoid saying 'No! You're wrong!" pg. 2).

The teaching session must be an enjoyable, active time for the student [and the teacher]; one they can look forward to each week with anticipation. This program has been designed with input from the students themselves. There are things for fingers to do, problems to be solved, and importantly, silly things to laugh at, for laughter is memorable.

Above all, this program leads from success to success, because the program is different enough to arouse their interest and to inspire them to listen.

2. <u>The student must understand the process,</u> but should not have to memorise either rules or spellings. The aim of the program is that the student will come to think about words for themselves. From hearing sounds, writing words, and understanding some basic "rules" for constructing words, the student then goes on to build word families and compile individual lists of useful words. After this work, the student will be thinking more purposefully and confidently about words, and then the formal reading of text can begin. Of course, reading has been going on all the time at the word level, but no development of sequential meaning has been involved, and the student has not thought of it as reading.

Students of average or higher intelligence usually progress quickly using this method, while students with learning difficulties and more complex reading and spelling problems can move slowly through the program at their own pace to achieve success. Though developed as an individual teaching method, it is adaptable to classroom use and has been used with success, in both infant and primary classes as part of the normal reading program, as well as in special classes as part of a remediation program with primary and secondary grades. Any remedial work is best done individually, but where necessary, can be achieved using small groups (2-5 is the best number). Work with larger groups is difficult because of the individuality of the students' reading problems, their differing stages of development and the teachers need to provide focused one on one support for each student.

Finally, this is a hands-on program and was developed through the practical experience gained from years of working with a multitude of reasons as to why each student struggled to conquer the barrier to their success when reading and spelling. It will only be fully appreciated as teachers and parents put it into practice, making modifications to suit their own, and their pupils' strengths and limitations.

The program consists of four parts: Exploring; Decoding; Discovering; and Building, and is presented as it would be used in individual teaching. Teachers wishing to use it with whole classes should consult Appendix 3: "Adaptations for whole class work".

Summary of Outcomes

In Part 1, the student will:

1. Understand the concept of a "sound" in a spoken word, and its relationship with a letter in a written word;
2. Be able to sound out and write simple consonant, vowel, consonant words;
3. Improve handwriting skills, where necessary. (see Appendix 1, p. 150).

In Part 2, the student will:

1. Focus on Auditory – listening for new and different sounds in words
2. Master coordination in auditory and motor skills – "Talk to Pencil"
3. Create their own Decoding Book to build word families and "put away" spelling list words on appropriate pages (in preparation for more advanced work using Jenny's Sound Dictionary – Section 2 p. 79).

The Importance of Intervention

Helping children and adults with a reading problem takes understanding and time. Like overcoming the sound barrier seemed insurmountable for the aeronautical engineers in the late 1940's, overcoming, the reading barrier seems insurmountable to some children and holds them back from meeting typical reading, writing and spelling milestones. Fortunately, like the sound barrier, the reading barrier can be conquered with patience, persistence and the right intervention support.

Insufficient recognition is given to the enormous achievement of pre-school children in acquiring skills of oral communication. The sudden barrier, the need to convert the sounds they hear into mysterious written symbols in order to gain access to the wonderful universe of knowledge beyond, can for a child be a devastating experience.

If this were a mechanical problem we could solve it easily by designing and manufacturing a new robotic model. Life is not so easy. As with all life, the child's growth depends on creating a favourable environment and giving the right kind of stimuli. Like blossoms budding on a fruit tree in spring, the child's mind opens to warmth, sunshine and frolicsome breezes; shrivels and withers in frost, and drops off in hail.

The child's self-confidence and natural zest for growth is defeated by inability to read, by a history of failures, by the scorn of companions, and by the worrying concern of adults. This may, and often does, result in negative attitudes to learning-inattention ("I can't" and "I don't care"), disruptive behaviour ("and huh to you too!"), and dropout ("I hate reading, hate school, hate, hate, hate"). This program aims at early intervention to help children overcome the reading barrier. Additionally, the interventions within its method will also help youth and adults who continue to struggle with reading and spelling. As students gain the ability to hear a sound and make the connection with its written symbol the reading barrier starts to break down.

Identifying Different Kinds of Reading Difficulty

By observing children attempting to read, a teacher can, in most cases, identify the kind of problem they are having and explain it to them. This is a most important part of the correction of reading difficulties, because through it, the child is helped to accept the difficulty and work positively towards eliminating it. The diagrams following are an attempt to illustrate some common kinds of reading problems, from the reader's point of view. (See also Appendix 5). Look at the diagrams yourself, then read the text. When you understand them, go through them with your student. The idea is to help the student to think about the way they are processing print when spelling or reading. Is it that they want to read but have little or no connection between the symbols on the page and the sounds they hear in speech, or is it something else?

Simply, three things are involved in reading: vision (visual sensation - first you see it), perception (visual perception - comprising registering, understanding, decoding and interpreting what is seen *connecting the letter/symbol and sound relationships in your head*), and the motor mechanism that will produce the sounds represented by what is seen and how it is perceived and interrupted. A more sophisticated analysis would include auditory processing, but this will mostly be dealt with by working on sounds (phonics). The basic elements, then, are:

READING

Preception

Vision

Motor Mechanism

I am going to read

Fig. 1

Nearly all poor readers and non-readers have a desire to read. For some, the attempt has for so long been a frustrating experience that it is now covered up by apparent indifference or even antagonism towards reading. But basically, children want to read. Remedial teachers, parents and others helping children [or adults] to read must believe so, and go on believing it despite initial appearances to the contrary.

Fig 2: To a child, however, they look and feel like this:

I am going to read

Fig. 2

Occasionally, of course, one encounters the child who just will not try at all, despite our best efforts. Sometimes we may be so intent ourselves that we on what he is supposed to be doing that we do not see that he is not even looking, and we wonder why he doesn't succeed. Observe the child continually to evaluate response and progress.

There is also a very small percentage of children who appear intelligent and willing and yet for whom reading is not a possibility. They need diagnosis of a kind that only a neurologist or reading clinic can offer, for it seems that they are able to make no sense of print at all. Perhaps they will never read. They are a small percentage of problem readers, however, but their problems are real, and may result from visual perceptual difficulties that need expert diagnosis and treatment.

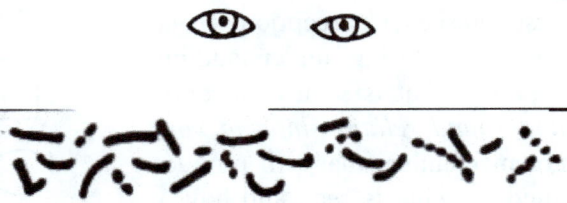

I cannot understand

Fig. 3

Fig. 3: The student here maybe knows the spoken word is made up of sounds but they have no perception [concept or realisation] that the sounds they hear in words are represented in each of the funny symbols [or letters in the alphabet] they see all over the page in front of them.

I Can See ...

Oh!

What is it?

Fig. 4

Fig. 4: Most children fall into the general category represented by this diagram.

The various kinds of problems under this general picture are shown in Figs. 5a, 5b, 5c, and 5d. In these cases, the child sees the print satisfactorily, wishes to read it, perhaps even expects to be able to read it, but somewhere between the eyes and the brain the message gets confused. What the teacher has to find out is just where the process in breaking down.

If this cannot be ascertained, it may not be possible to fix up the reading. In the first kind of visual confusion, the child sees the words well enough, but has no regular habits of observation. His eyes jump anywhere and observe at random. Consequently he makes no sense, (or nonsense), of what he reads. In most cases, he has not been taught the discipline of invariable left-to-right observation, and has had little or no training in phonics. (See below, Reading Checkpoint 10, p. 68). It may also be that the child has problems with eyetracking because of muscle imbalance, or because of sensitivity to the contrast of the white page and the black print. In the second kind of visual confusion (fig. 5b), the child again sees the words clearly, but has an unreliable visual memory.

He tries to use his memory, feels the pressure of time, panics, and is unable to attempt a systematic analysis of the word he originally saw correctly. In spelling, this is the child who writes eeg for egg.

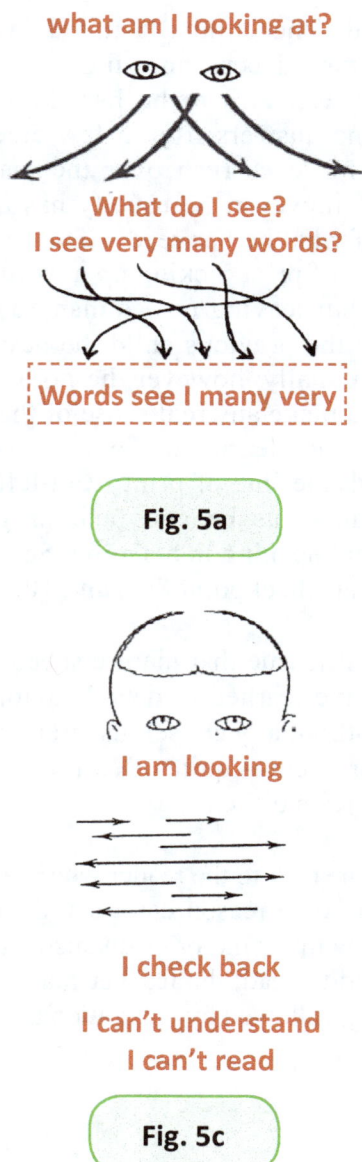

"I remember a double letter, I remember the e and the g —what was the double? — Oh! — I must write something (panic) ..."

The next child sees the words correctly, and his eyes move fairly well across the page, but he lacks confidence and checks back continually:

The underlying cause is usually lack of confidence.

The result is hesitation at least, confusion almost certainly, failure to read and understand at worst, because of a complete loss of the sequence of words and ideas.

Fig. 5d: The child illustrated in the next figure would perform quite well on speed reading tests where he has the chance of guessing answers from a few clues picked up as his eyes rush over the material. In reality, however, he usually has almost no idea of what he has read. His eyes run over the line of print picking up a word here and there, but leaving out as many as he sees. Unlike the previous child, he never checks back. Usually, however, he notices insufficient to make any real sense of the passage. He has not learnt to move systematically through the line of print from left to right, "decoding" as he goes and progressively forming meaning in his mind. See p. 67–68, Reading Checkpoint 8(b) and 10.

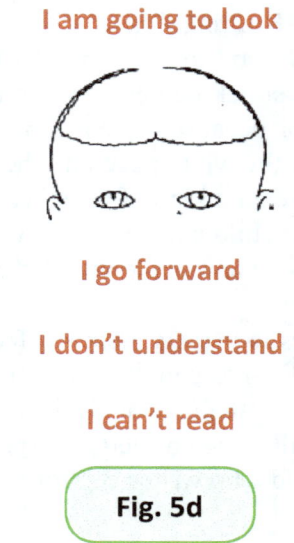

I am going to look

I go forward

I don't understand

I can't read

Fig. 5d

While it is true that mature speed readers use this kind of strategy, it is also true that they have learned to decode automatically, so that they can process the words fast, and without any conscious attention to the task. That is very different from this child. This problem is quite often found in intelligent secondary pupils. It makes success in all subjects difficult.

We come now to the reader who sees the words correctly and appears to understand them, but for some reason can't say them correctly. It appears as though there is something wrong with the motor mechanism, though the cause may be emotional. When such a pupil is asked to read, the teacher may observe anticipation, even pleasure at the prospect of reading, followed by frustration as "it won't come out":

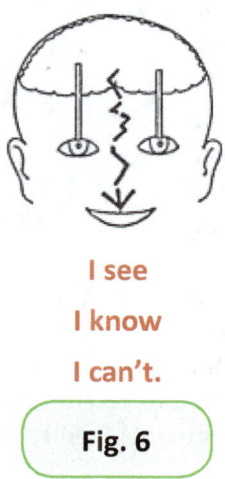

I see

I know

I can't.

Fig. 6

Motor mechanism
(Tell me what it's about)

As soon as possible such a child must read silently, and not be forced to read aloud at all. He will probably make very little use of the auditory channel in reading. Where possible, encourage oral reading after preparation through silent reading. (See also Reading Checkpoint 9, p. 67)

The child in Fig. 7 has used his eyes to see the words, and his mouth reads fairly well. Unaccountably, words are mispronounced so that "the ears can make no real sense of the reading". He may, for example, read a sentence quite well but substitute *exclaim* for *explain,* or *tephelone* for *telephone,* making it difficult for him to get the meaning of the sentence. This problem reveals a basic auditory processing difficulty.

I can't see but...

Fig. 7

In such cases, detailed work will be needed on visual discrimination of words and letters, emphasizing at the same time left-to-right eye movements. Controlled flashcard reading of word groups like very every, ever; explain, exclaim, except, will be needed, the emphasis being on sequential sound analysis. Write these words (well spaced) anywhere on a page as a first exercise, then, cut the page up into cards and scatter them on a table for checking and comparison before reading them as flash cards. When a page of text has been read, words mispronounced should be located and re-read, with emphasis on structural analysis. (Cover part of the word and have the child observe and say the part he mispronounced. Add this to the rest of the word, and say the whole word).

In the next case, (Fig.8), the child's pronunciation is right, but still there is little or no understanding of what has been read. At worst, the words just come out "like beads on a string", all of equal value, without phrasing or expression. At best, this reading is fairly fluent, but some of the pauses are in the wrong places. The decoding process is performed quite well, but the concepts represented by the words are not retained nor related to other concepts in the passage. This problem is usually fixed quite easily by teaching the child where to pause in reading, and helping him to be sure that the first two words after stopping are always right. (See Reading Checkpoints 3 and 4, p. 65–66) Lastly, we look at a child who is a good reader.

I read well but...

Fig. 8

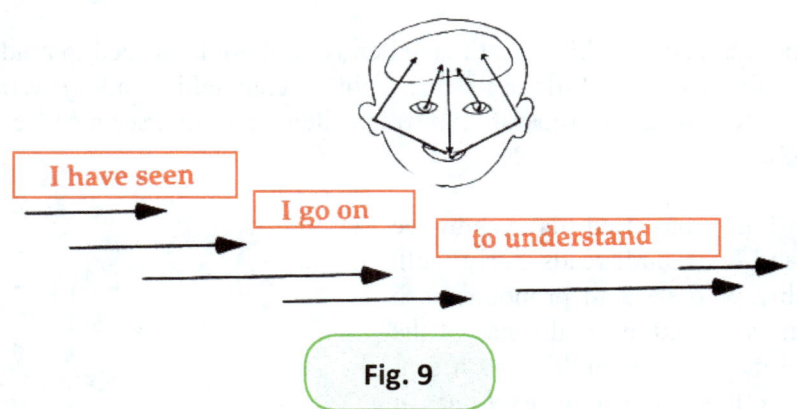

Fig. 9

In the early stages the "ears" are involved, both in decoding and interpreting, but as speed increases the ears and mouth are both eliminated from the reading process, and the decoding takes place silently and automatically in the brain. A child like this one needs assistance mainly in increasing speed of reading. and when to adjust reading speed. For example, when reading silently speed does not matter, but when reading aloud to an audience the speed must be adjusted to ensure diction is clear and audible.

> Appendix 5 provides a chart of the illustrations used in this chapter, for use in discussing different ways of processing with your student. It is important that the student understands from the beginning how processing should occur, and is constantly encouraged to monitor their own way of processing.

Part 1

Exploring Letter/Sound Connections

ACTIVITY PLAN
Discovering Reading and Spelling through Sound

ACTIVITY	1	2	3	4	5	6	7
SOUND CHARTS	The beginning SOUND	Consonants & Vowels	Revision – Make your own vowel charts	Both charts displayed for reference			
Discovering Rd & Sp Through Sounds TUTORS Handbook [Page REFERENCES for each Activity]			Listening 1 sound, 2 sounds	Talk to Pencil	Danger Vowels & Bossy 'e'	'e' or 'I'	Double Letters
RECORDING		For each individual – record activity dialog for later revision. Add additional words for later individual work.					
SPELLING LISTS			Make your own writing chart	Words from school lists can be spelt using the rules so far taught, or using "talk-to-the-pencil" principle.			
DECODING BOOK [Student activity]				Begin your own Start to 'put away' important words and do a little word building.			
READING	Provide support and reassurance as auditory skills grow, sound/word connections start to make sense and words are spoken with accurate sound pronunciation.						
JENNY'S SOUND DICTIONARY	The Student begins to build up word families according to their sounds.						

Part 1: Exploring Letter/Sound Connections

8	9	10	11	12	13	14	15	16	17
Also make Safe & Danger Vowel Chart available for reference									
'c'&'k'	'c'&'k' to finish	'k' only 1 friend	'c' only 1 friend	When 'g' says 'jjj'					
Record activities plus additional words.					Make "x-plan" recordings based on spelling lists. Periodic "Z-oom" recordings for revision.				
					Begin "detective pages". Intensive work on word families based on words from weekly spelling lists.				
					Begin oral reading. Analyse problems (see page 60). Teach how to use the "PUSHER" for fluency (see page 116).				

Activity 1: Preliminary Work With Younger Children

The beginning – SOUND

Let us begin at the beginning, with the sounds a child uses in naming what they see. This part links sight to sound, and then to the letter-symbol. For example, a picture of a cat, to a /k/ sound, to the printed word 'cat'. It will help the student discover basic letter/sound relationships, it teaches them to listen for and identify sounds, to distinguish the differences between the snap of consonants and the breath blow of vowels. We need to establish a smooth flow between the sound students hear and the symbol they "tell" their pencil to write. The student never has to learn, to memorise by rote. The process is one of discovery, and of the development of perception and action skills. From the beginning the student is listening, converting, writing, and then checking back the written word against the sounds they have heard.

Working with preschoolers and kinders

Before Part 1 in this program, Preschoolers and Kinders in their learning activities would use the pictures/sounds/letters/words supplied for Part 1, and be introduced slowly at the teacher's discretion, to the consonant charts (see p. 21). These pictures would finally be positioned on one of the charts in preparation for Part 1. Use a large scrap book/exercise book. Draw well spaced lines for the children's guidance writing in. Letters, which may have been practised by tracing earlier, have pictures to match the sounds being written. Right

Common Confusions

1. **b** and **d**
   Write h and turn it into a b as you do. Say "/h/-to-/b/" as you write. Or use the "The boy filled his belly, h to b" mnemonic (see the Consonant Chart – boy eating apple).

2. **g** and **j**
   See the girl on the Consonant chart sitting on her long hair so that the boys won't pull it!

3. **s** (directional confusion)
   Start like the little "cat /k/" and then chase the snake around.

4. **/f/ & /th/** {pronunciation confusion} f is for fish. When you go fishing, you need a ... hook! So hook your top teeth over your bottom lip to say /f/. /th/ is the rude one: you poke out your tongue to say it properly. Practise using tongue-twisters (see the Sound Dictionary under "th").

5. **m/n**
   For /m/ you have your two lips closed (looks like an m on its side) so put two loops. For /n/, you have your lips open, so only put one loop.

6. **p** (position on line)
   The pig has his feet in the mud, and his head on the ground (i.e. on the line).

handers would need to think about the work the left hand has to do; The first task is to hold down the page or book, the second to ensure left-to-right direction. The left hand "talks" to the right hand and says "go away"→ "move a way from me". This can help with letters such as, **Z**→ The zoo is over there.

→; **C** ..where the initial direction is R-L: "The cat is coming the wrong way! Go back!"(←). Some letters require other clues, eg. p, whose descender goes below the line, is for that reason, difficult. Small children like this clue: The pig has "feet in the mud - head on the ground". Reverse directions for left handers. See also Appendix 1, Writing Revision.

Capital letters should not be introduced at this early stage. Names of letters in the alphabet should be avoided at this stage (exception; danger vowels). These names contain more than one sound, they do not blend, and cannot be the basis for early reading. Focus therefore, on the sound of the letter.

"Sight words" as a method, is not advisable as many students have poor visual recall and many short words are similar in shape. For optimum progress, the student must achieve at every level. In learning to write by sounds, the student is actually learning the elements of reading from the very beginning.

<u>Part 1 of the program is concerned with simple sounds</u>, their basic symbols, and how to print out the word that is heard. By the end of Part 1 the student can read simple words even if they have never seen them in writing before.

Most school age and adult students will already be able to write, but a revision section on handwriting is included in case this is needed to enhance current ability, build confidence. Improving handwriting skills is also a good way reinforce decoding of simple and tricky letter/sound connections for the kinesthetic learner (see Appendix 1).

<u>In Part 2 students create their very own sound dictionary</u>, your "Decoding Book" (including Part 1); (where the student cracks the code). In making this book they learn, in a hands-on practical way, that letters are not always what they seem. Letter "c" is for "city" as well as for "cat"; /s/ as well as /k/. Of course there is also the letter s and the letter k. What to use where and why is the problem, and how to remember?

It is in this section that the relationship between teacher and pupil becomes a vital learning factor. Learning is a discovery, and the student is the discoverer. The teacher-pupil link is that of guide and climber on a mountaineering expedition. The student is safe, and goes forward fearlessly, knowing the teacher will keep him or her from error. Through this section it is also critical to maintain the practical, hands on approach to learning, engaging the three main sensory receivers – auditory, visual and kinesthetic styles which the student will use to learn and grow. The creation of the Decoding Book is about ownership of learning for the student, face to face engagement for the teacher, a partnership that involves discussing, searching, cutting, pasting, talking, observing, rewarding, colouring, writing, practicing, supporting, listening and reflecting.

Every teacher knows that the place to begin is exactly where that student is up to. So, if an older or adult student knows only the alphabet names of letters, and is unfamiliar with the sounds, the SOUND is where these students will have to start. Only then can their studies bear fruit quickly. Their search is for a speedy recovery in skills - offer this speedy recovery and they will co-operate willingly in the program exactly as it is. Treat Part 1as a "warming up session", for stimulation.

Rules are to be discovered, not learned by rote. Apt phrases and pictures will fasten them in memory. The students "talk to their pencil" and test what they have discovered in new words, which can be read knowledgeably. The process is sound-and-letter based and developed through familiarity with rules in practical use: the student becomes a good writer as well as a good reader, able to spell correctly, a person skilled in words.

For every session, there are pictures, or a chart to show. The rhythm of the session is that the child See, Question, Discover and Try Out. Throughout, the teacher gives encouragement and praise.

In concluding each session, the teacher is also given the opportunity to confirm what has been learned. It would be a good idea for the student to make a list of the things they have learnt. Perhaps the first page of the new Decoding Book could look like this:

I have learned about		
Stage		Page
1	Listening – one sound, two sounds	1
2		3
3		5
4		7
5		9

It will also be useful to set up a simple follow-up activity, and to look forward to continuing the delightful discovery game at the next session.

Key Elements for Teacher to Consider:

As the teacher, I am there to facilitate the child's discovery of their own adventure into the world of letters, sounds, words, spelling and reading.

Will my technique be:

DIFFERENT enough to arouse

INTEREST? Will it make the student

LISTEN? Is it within their

ABILITY to take up the

CHALLENGE of independent

REASONING? Will they make

DISCOVERIES? Will they lead them quickly to

SUCCESS? Be sure they are always

RIGHT. Never wrong. Be sure to follow the pattern.

BE PARTNERS

How to avoid using the phrase "Sound it Out"

The word 'sound' to your student represents any sound, a vibration registered by his ears. It probably does not convey anything specific in relation to the structure of a word. At the least, there is almost certainly a confusion between the 'sound' of the letter and its alphabetical name. This is not helped by the fact that, for the vowel, one of the sounds they represent is also their name!

Talk about what the letters 'sound'. This avoids the confusion with the alphabetic name (which is a series of sounds). Teach the student – "you just say what the letter says".

Activity 2: Discovering Consonant and Vowels Sounds

Note: It is important to stick to the scripted language below. That is because a critical part of the success of the Lamond Method was based on the standard language script Jenny developed and used consistently.

a. The Consonants Sounds

Aim: To develop familiarity and memory of consonants through sight, sound and symbol presentation and practice in games.

Preparation: Consonant chart with pictures. Consonant chart with letters only. Consonant chart with words.

Blank squares chart [Chart Templates - Appendix 6 (Activity 20)]

- Position of picture
- Sound of first letter
- Sound of first letter, link sound to picture and "READ"
- For games

Procedure:

1st Game: TEACHER'S QUESTION — STUDENT RESPONSE

Using picture side of chart, one row at a time. Points, using pointer.
Where is ...? (Naming a picture.)
Game continues, row by row at teacher's discretion.
Student commended for success.

2nd Game: Using picture side of chart. ...Names the picture.
Which picture am I thinking about? N.B....No pointing!
(...Naming first sound of picture.)

3rd Game: Using letter side of chart. Where should the ...(naming picture) be? Points, using a pointer
Where is ...(naming a sound of a letter)?

4th Game: Using letter side of chart: Names the sound
What does this say?...(Pointing to letter)

5th Game: Using blank chart and cut up cards.
Teacher's Supportive Questions... What can you remember?
Can you remember anything about where the pictures should be? Where was the cat? Place the cat. What about the snake? The lamp? What else? Very good.

6th Game: Using cut up cards put letters in correct places and say the sound.

7th Game: Using cut up cards put words in correct places, reading the words.

Final Question: WHAT HAVE YOU LEARNED TODAY?

If you use laminated sheet, students can take them home and use them as place mats. Knowing the position of the pictures is important for later recall of what the letters 'say'. Always have the chart available as a support.

Consonant Picture Chart (giving the sound of the letter)

Consonant Letter Chart

c	d	g	j	ch
s	r	n	m	sh
l	t	h	b	th
f	k	p	x	qu
v	y	w	z	wh

Consonant Word Chart

cat	dog	girl	jug	church
snake	rabbit	nest	mouse	shoe
lamp	tent	hat	boy	three
fish	kitten	pig	box	queen
van	yacht	web	zebra	whistle

b. The 'Safe' Vowels Sounds

> **General Principles:**
>
> (See Figure 10, next page) For chart Templates of pictures, letters for student activities see Appendix 6
>
> Follow directions provided — should reinforcement in skill with this chart be needed, provide a blank chart, pictures and letters for games or exercises.
> Then; without removing supportive charts, write first by sounds, then by saying whole words, some of the listed words, referring back to Charts when necessary.
>
> **Alternative activities**
>
> For students having difficulty in writing, letter cards could be used to "make" words, instead of just writing words.
>
> Have a supply of letter cards and invent games.
>
> Timing with a stop-watch would be an added challenge.
>
> * ENCOURAGE AND SUPPORT; DO NOT TEST.

Aim: Students will know the difference between vowels and consonants and readily write one syllable words using the five basic vowels, which are 'safe' in spelling.
Preparation: Give each student a Safe Vowel Chart and a sheet of lined paper for writing.
Procedure:

QUESTION:	What's the difference between a vowel and a consonant? (A consonant snaps, a vowel blows).
ACTION:	Try this out with each of the pictures.
	What's the first? An apple. a Blowing sound blow .... a-a-a-a. Try the next. An egg. e Blow .... e-e-e-e.
	In the same way blow for i, o, u.
QUESTION:	Why do you think we call these sounds 'safe'?
	(Because these sounds are short blows – short vowels – easy to start – no complications.
	The light is GREEN – it's "safe".)
ACTION:	Why not put a green box around them? Green for safety?
	Have you a green pen there?

Using the Safe Vowel Chart

TEACHER'S QUESTIONS

1st Game
Where is .... Naming the picture.

2nd Game
Which picture am I thinking about? Naming a sound.

3rd Game
(Reverse Side) What does this say? Pointing to letter.

STUDENT RESPONSE

1st Game
Student points to picture with pointer.

2nd Game
Student names the picture. No pointing.

3rd Game
(Reverse Side) Student says the sound.

Fig. 10

Write these words, or make these words with letter cards, first by sounds then by saying whole words.

a		e		i		o		u	
and	that	bed	them	sit	grin	hot	frog	fun	just
bag	cash	get	text	hid	chin	lot	lost	but	plum
cap	ramp	ten	step	fin	swim	rod	stop	cup	much
dab	trap	yes	then	tip	limp	jog	trot	mug	drum
fan	swam	met	sled	dim	list	top	cost	bus	jump
gap	grand	hem	crept	hit	strip	got	from	gum	brush
jam	clamp	peg	chest	dig	print	mob	cloth	mud	rub
had	smash	pen	fresh	him	swish	box	frost	cut	trust
bat	ranch	net	shelf	fix	twist	log	comet	hug	lunch
tab	stamp	leg	swept	zip	chimp	nod	throb	pup	stump
rag		men		in		job	crops	sun	
sat		jet		big		mop		tub	
tap		web		mix		fox		but	
van		end		lid		dog		bud	
band		best		mint		pop		dust	
crab		shed		flip		shop		shut	
dash		next		dish		pond		pump	
clap		west		slid		soft		rush	
flag		mesh		rich		spot		club	

Part 2

Decoding Words

Creating the Decoding Book. Once the basic sounds are known, the student then learns to put the letter/sound connections together to make words. Making their own Decoding Book supports the learning of new sound/letter combinations, develops understanding of their rules, and records what has been learnt for future reference. In further developing the student's understanding of this, we will construct a Decoding Book that records what has been learnt, and is always available to remind the student. For young children this may take the form of a scrapbook, while older children will use an exercise book of about 20 to 30 pages. Seniors may prefer to use a small loose-leaf [A5] ring binder.

Activity 3: Introduction to the Decoding Book

Part 2 of the Lamond Method is based around student engagement by making their own Decoding Book and is key to the effectiveness of the program. In this part students complete set activities in listening, looking, decoding and recording what they are learning in their Decoding Book. The guided activities are set out on the following pages.

In the back half of the Decoding Book the students will build their own Sound Dictionary containing tricky word families that have similar sounds and different letter combinations. For example, when they decode a sound/letter combination they find tricky, such as /ch/ in church. In the Sound Dictionary [section] of their Decoding Book they write the sound 'ch' on a new page and the word 'church' under it. Then they spend time thinking about the word and finding (or drawing) a picture of a church beside the word. Next, they think about other words that have the same /ch/ sound in them and add them to the page under the word church.

Over time, as they discover new words that belong to a word family, such as /ch/ they can go back and add them to that page [eg. chocolate, chop etc.]. Later, as the student progress to Parts 3 and 4, they will add new word families to their Sound Dictionary such as the air/ere/eir/are/etc. families or the or/ar/aw/awe/etc. families]

The student should be encouraged to cover the book and label one side John's Decoding Book and the flip side John's Sound Dictionary.

Listening – One Sound? Two Sounds?

Note: It is important to stick to the scripted language below, as a critical part of the success of the Lamond Method was based on the standard language script Jenny developed and used.

Aim: To develop Auditory Skills.
Preparation: Students Decoding Book, pictures (see Appendix 7), pens – green, red and black, ruler, scissors, glue.
Procedure:
1. This is a listening page. You are going to do four things and I am only going to tell you once (with actions), so listen.
2. a. Draw a margin.
   b. Divide the page in half (across, with Tutor's hand vertical).
   c. Glue a red circle in top half, draw round it with red pen.
   d. Glue star in the lower half

3. Tell me what you have done.

4. That is a funny way to start a listening page, isn't it?

5. Now are you ready to listen?

6. Beside the red circle write the sound /r/. It is round and red.

7. Beside the blue star write the sound you hear for /ar/.

8. (Students usually write 'r' again for /ar/.)

9. Listen again, this time with eyes closed. Say /r/ and /ar/.
   Do they sound the same, or are they different?

10. Listen /r/ – How many sounds in a quick /r/ - one or two? Write "1" in the margin.

11. Listen again /ar/. How many sounds in /ar/ – one or two?
    (Students usually repeat 1, because they visualise the alphabet letter.)

12. At the bottom of the page write the word 'car'.

13. Cover the first letter with your left thumb, cover the rest of the word with your other thumb.

14. Now lift your left thumb. What does that letter say? (Reply should be, "That letter says /k/ (sound)" Good, recover k.

15. Lift your other thumb. What sound this time? Reply – /ar/.

16. But you told me a minute ago that one letter (pointing to 'r' beside the star) said /ar/. Which one really says /ar/?

17. (Students usually persist that the one letter 'r' says /ar/.)

18. Again at the bottom of the page, write the word 'car' without the middle letter. Does that say 'car'? No, that says /cr/. So /ar/ has two letters and two sounds. Write two in the margin.

19. Using a scrap of paper write sounds heard in /em/, then /m/. (Students usually write 'm' for both.)

20. Listen again, this time with eyes closed. /em/, /m/. Do they sound the same, or are they different?

21. (Use covering technique to prove a sound is missing.)

22. Now let's try /es/ and /s/, /en/ and /n/, /el/ and /l/, /te/ and /t/ and /ar/ and r to discover which belong to one and which belong to two sounds.

23. Now let us put all this into your new Decoding Book.

24. In one sound section write the word 'snarl' – saying the sounds as you write.

25. If snarl was in your spelling list, would you learn it? Why would you need to learn it; didn't you get it right? Thumb check.

26. Now, if you are going to learn snarl, you are going to say, /es – en – ay – ar – el/. In two sound section write what you hear when you say *esenayarel*. How many letters? How many sounds?

27. Every letter in this word makes a sound, so you have too many sounds in your head when you 'learn' spelling words.

28. Which way is better, to say the word or to spell the word?

29. Practise words from the list – finishing with *splendid*.

30. Do you understand about listening to the sounds in words?

TUTOR'S WORD LISTS

One Sound

f	l	m	n	r	s
for	lamp	man	nod	ran	sand
from	lost	men	net	trust	stand
fish	clap	must	next	brush	sat
far	lid	mud	snag	trip	this
fun	lump	mop	snip	trap	rust
soft	land	jump	tin	ribs	snap
gift	until	rim	nut	rub	stunt
flat	lent	jam	nun	print	sunset
if	lift	smash	fan	grunt	stamp
finish	lunch	map	pond	crab	step

Two Sound

ef	el	em	en	ar	es	x=/ks/	x=/ks/
left	self	them	then	far	west	text	fix
deft	elf	stem	spend	arm	test	next	lax
cleft	felt	lemon	lend	star	rest	extra	mix
heft	shelf	hem	mend	garden	best	extend	tax
	help	hemp	hen	arch	escort	flex	six
	belt	tempo	tent	target	crest	expo	ox
	melt	tempest	pen	cart	chest	vex	flax
	spelt	ember	send	smart	yes	extend	relax
	elm	member	den	farm	nest	expand	box
				march	zest		fox

Activity 4: Talk to your Pencil

Aim: To develop concentration and co-ordination in auditory and oral techniques with motor skills using 'head charts'.

Preparation: Teacher: Head charts, (see Appendix 5).

Student: 5 pictures for page 31 (see opposite), scissors, glue, Students Decoding Book, ruler, pens.

Procedure:

1. Directed to the student – Do you ever talk to your pencil? No? Just have a look at these charts. They show a person writing words.
2. The words are travelling. Which way are they moving in each chart?
3. Are they different?
4. (a) Which way do you choose when you are writing your words?

    (b) When you hear a word, which way does it travel? Choose the chart you think would be right for the way you write your words. (Discuss each chart as it is selected.)
5. Chart 'C'? That's a popular one.
6. Let us use chart 'C' and write 'contented'. Good.
7. Ah, one problem, I saw your mouth move – look at chart 'C', the mouth isn't used.
8. Chart 'C' can't be right, let's throw it away – think again.
9. 'A'? We will use chart 'A'. Which way does this word travel? It looks a slow route. Do you have lots of time to write your words at school? No? Is 'A' the right chart? Choose again.
10. 'D'? Good. Why don't you like chart 'B?' Is it too slow? Is the mouth used?
11. 'D'. Why is this one right? Does it say the word clearly and quickly? So you do talk to your pencil.
12. Directed to the teacher/parent-tutor – Students do not understand the term "Sound it out" (refer to 'Sound it out' explanation back on page 19). Instead, use the expressions. "Say the word", "Talk to pencil".
13. Using chart 'D', demonstrate the route the sounds travel from ear to pencil, by writing the word 'content' c-o-n-t-e-n-t.
14. Student checks own work by covering the word with the right thumb and slowly sliding thumb away, blending sounds as letters appear, so that the written word is read. Praise.
15. Use talk to pencil procedure from listed words until writing even longer words in syllables becomes automatic and the student is confident and successful. (Longer 'safe' words are listed in Appendix 4.)

16. Now, on a new page in your Decoding Book, glue in the cut out pictures provided (Appendix 5). Fill in the correct route on the blank picture. From the list write words on page 32.

17. Homework – write words from the list. Say the word you write, then cover and say the word again as you move your finger along to check. N.B. "Talk to Pencil Words" have no catches.

Final Question: WHAT DID YOU LEARN ON THESE TWO PAGES?

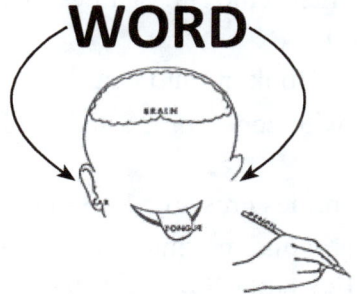

Which way does the **Word** travel?

Think and **Choose**.

Draw in the **Word** travelling to your pencil.

TEACHER'S PAGE　　　**STUDENT'S PAGE**

1a　　　　　　　　　　　1b

What did you learn?

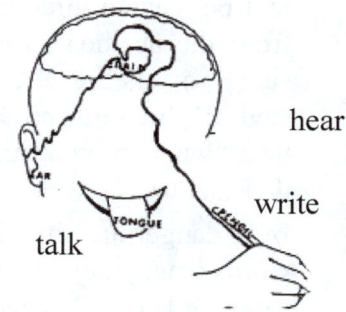

WORD

talk

Talk to Pencil

I say the word slowly as I write, then I cover and say the word again as I slide my finger along to check.

Part 2: Decoding Words

Activity 5: Safe and Danger Vowels (Emergency) 'E'

Aim: To strengthen auditory concentration and to introduce vowel chart as "Safe and Danger" Chart. (See Fig. 12.) p. 34

Preparation: Teacher – Coloured green and red vowel chart and pointer. Student – Safe and Danger Consonant chart (Appendix 6), Students Decoding Book, ruler, pens.

Procedure:

1. Using teacher's Safe & Danger chart and pointer, enjoy the games or exercises (see directions in teacher's reference, opposite).
2. Teacher copies Teacher's page 2 into Decoding Book or onto board.
3. Student numbers pages 2 and 3, rules page 3 with centre green and red lines like the chart.
4. Together look at Teacher's page 2, student identifies cross road, roundabout, etc.
5. Teacher draws parked truck, with safe vowels – one moving out into the line of traffic. This is a dangerous situation and causes an accident. All the vowels are thrown out of the car.
6. Discuss what will happen; who will come to control the traffic in this 'danger' situation emergency 'e'.
7. Place letter 'e' in roundabout to be the silent policeman directing the traffic away from the accident. Emergency e makes sure vowels are OK (which is the first step in first-aid procedure) by asking then "what are your names?" Vowels say their names.
8. In a dangerous situation or in 'danger' words emergency 'e' comes at the end. In safe words no 'e' is needed at the end.
9. Now for words. (Ensure the student has the Safe & Danger chart, green and red pens.)

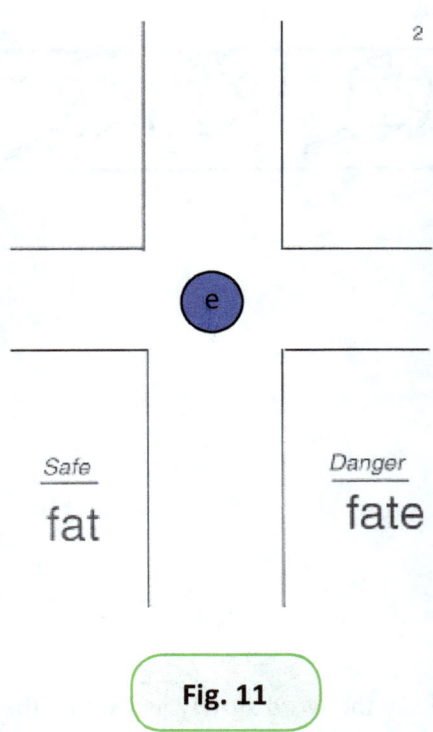

Fig. 11

10. Discuss significance of colours, green – safe, red – danger.
11. Use the following procedure to write the first word
    plan /a/   which picture? (refer chart)
                  green or red? (which pen?)
                  safe or danger? (which column?)
                  green-safe-talk to pencil >Plan
12. Repeat the same procedure for the second word.
    plane /ay/ which picture? (refer chart)
                  green or red? (which pen?)
                  safe or danger? (which column?)
                  red-danger-talk to pencil > plan
13. All students take some time to understand the pattern, so they favour stopping at letter "n". Encourage this with the following discussion.
14. Running commentary between teacher and student follows: Both words look alike. Student and teacher are surprised that both words sound different, but look alike.

    Which is which? Student suggests green says plan, red says plane, but what if you are colour blind? Now look last page (fig.11). Look Fig. 11 at the accident. Where is the emergency 'e'? Where is the danger word? Shouldn't the emergency 'e' be there?
15. Student finally realises that emergency 'e' is needed at the end of these danger words.
16. Practise words from lists, using same procedure (Step 13 or 14) for every word.
17. Proceed to longer words using ordinary pens and paper, always checking last sounding vowel for danger – emergency 'e' at the end of a word is a danger word.
18. Homework: Student to colour own Safe and Danger chart (green and red), mount on cardboard, protect with plastic and if possible, write more words from lists.

Final Question: WHAT DID YOU LEARN ON THESE TWO PAGES?

Safe & Danger Chart

TEACHER'S QUESTIONS	STUDENT'S RESPONSE
Green side first	Green side first
1st Game	**1st Game**
Where is .... (Naming the picture)	Student points to picture.
2nd Game	**2nd Game**
Which picture am I thinking about? (Naming a vowel sound)	Student names the picture. No pointing
Red side next	Red side next
Repeat both games	Repeat both games
Red & Green sides	Red & Green sides
Repeat games	Repeat games
3rd Game	**3rd Game**
No pointing No naming pictures Naming a sound... "Which colour?" "Safe or Danger?"	Only reply will be words "green or red" Student name colour Only "Safe" or Danger"

Fig. 12

Part 2: Decoding Words

TEACHER'S PAGE

STUDENT'S PAGE

fat	fate	timber	behave
rip	ripe	segment	invite
mad	made	credit	explode
hid	hide	melon	enclose
rod	rode	number	costume
pan	pane	nutmeg	volume
shin	shine	compost	value
rat	rate	member	confuse
Pip	pipe	barber	estate
can	cane	lotus	extreme
fine	twine	comet	unite
twin	nose	within	capsule
sap	came	slumber	refuse
then	cone	bunyip	athlete
them	those	tropic	complete
hit	side	titbit	advise
run	gale	tonic	escape
sit	hose	vanish	rescue
jump	these	pinup	grindstone
went	safe	trumpet	sunshine
yes	tame	velvet	provide
crab	wipe	plastic	depose
spot	fame	tulip	provide
flat	rose	wither	consume
twig	vine	poet	dilute
sun	name	tunic	migrate
glad	side	radish	impose
help	game	tiptop	brigade
hot			
	locust	tadpole	

Activity 6: Ending Sounds /e/ or /i/

Aim: To add to auditory skills, Thinking Strategies with Memory, in associating the same sounds with different letters.

Preparation: 2 pictures for pages 4 & 5 (See Appendix 6), scissors, glue, Students Decoding Book, ruler, pens.

Procedure:

1. Teacher copies Teacher's page 4 into the Decoding Book or onto board.
2. Student numbers pages 4 & 5, cuts out 2 pictures.
3. Directed to the student –
    a. Read the first line again. Which part of the words are you to notice especially on this page? (end.)
    b. So, which side of your page will have the margin? Good, draw the margin at the edge.
4. How many pictures did you cut out? So how many sections will you need? Good, divide the page.
5. Where are you going to glue the pictures? Why there? Any reason, or did your fingers just lay the pictures down? Where is the catch to be in these words? Where is the margin? Good, glue the pictures.
6. What are the pictures? BABY, FLY.
7. Say bab-ee, What is the last sound?
8. Shut your eyes -listen - bab-y-e -What do you hear?
9. In the margin, write what you hear last.
10. Lock up that /e/ so 'e' cannot escape.
11. Now, talk to pencil, and write this word: mem-or-y. (Students usually write 'e' at the end)
12. Ah, look in the margin. 'e' is locked up. Look back at page 1.
13. Try another word: nav-y. 'e'? No?
14. How about writing 'baby' (break through word).
15. Good, that's right. You didn't use 'e' that time; what did you use?
16. What about 'navy', 'memory'? Good. You are a good thinker.
17. Let's write some more words from the list. (Support the student by saying, "At the end, hearing e put…")
18. What about the FLY section? (Repeat procedure from 7., by using fly: /i/ - lock up the 'i'.
19. Write the words 'satisfy', 'magnify'. No?

20. How about writing my (break through word). Good.
21. You didn't use i. What did you use? 'Y'
22. Let us write more words from the list. Very Good.
23. Now, we are ready to fill in the margin.
24. 'e' is locked up – what did you use instead? 'Y'

    'i' is locked up – what did you use instead? 'Y' Write "y" in the margin. e, i, y help each other and are friends.
25. Now complete Teacher's page – Very good.

Final Question: WHAT DID YOU LEARN ON THESE TWO PAGES?

TEACHER'S PAGE	STUDENT'S PAGE
4 At the END of words, hearing sounds _____ or _____ you mostly put the letter _____	5
At the END of words seeing _____ you mostly say _____ or _____	

Part 2: Decoding Words

/ee/ sound = y	"Break-through" word = baby	
navy	empty	memory
cosy	partly	charity
pony	frosty	property
very	rugby	properly
tiny	costly	argosy
lily	hardy	stupidly
dusty	handy	victory
gusty	jumpy	stupidity
gravy	clumsy	monopoly
party	entry	ability
	slowly	

/i/ sound = y	"Break-through" word = my	
cry	deny	satisfy
fry	defy	magnify
try	imply	gratify
fly	reply	multiply
dry		testify
ply		modify
spry		simplify
why		verify

> Note: The words listed below are rarely a problem.

me	pie
see	tie
key	die

> Note to the teacher: Check student development at this stage. Is the student listening? thinking? risk-taking? joining in? anticipating? (not guessing).

Activity 7: Double Letters and Swimming Pools

Aim: To further develop Auditory Skills and Thinking Strategies in two syllable words.

Preparation: Three pictures for Pages 6 & 7 (Appendix 6), scissors, glue, Students Decoding Book, ruler, pens, Safe & Danger chart.

Procedure:

1. Teacher copies teacher's Page 6 into Decoding Book or onto board.
2. Student numbers Pages 6 & 7, cuts out pictures for page 7, rules Safe & Danger lines, draws Safe & Danger swimming pools.
3. Directed to the student – Let's look at the Teacher's Page 6 – it says 1 or 2?, 2 or 1?
4. What does the teacher want you to do with the three swimmers?
5. Well, look at the pools. Yes! The teacher wants you to decide where to put the one swimmer and where to put the two swimmers.
6. Would one swimmer ever be safe alone? No, one would be in danger, so, where would you put the one swimmer?
7. Would two together be safe? Where would you put the two swimmers?
8. Glue swimmers to correct pools.
9. At the top of the safe side write either one or two.
10. At the top of the danger side write the other number.
11. Why did you write the numbers where you did? (Students often write 1 and 2 in that correct sequence, without thinking about the significance of the page, with swimmers and pools. This question quickly rouses them!)
12. We are ready for words.
13. Do you have your Safe & Danger chart, green pen, and red pen?
14. The first word is 'hopping', from one side of the pool to the other.

    /o / which picture? (chart)... green or red? (pen)... safe or danger? (pool) Good! 'Hopping' is a safe word – now, Talk to Pencil (T.T.P.)!

    On one side of the pool 'ho', in the pool 'p', other side of the pool, 'ing'. Remember safe word – how many times is 'p' in the pool?

15. The second word is 'hoping'

    'o' which picture? (chart) green or red? (pen) safe or danger? (pool) Good! 'Hoping' is a danger word – now T.T.P.

    On one side of the pool, 'ho', in the pool, 'p', other side of the pool, 'ing' Remember – danger word – how many times is 'p' in the pool?

16. Let's do some more words from the lists. Keep your chart there to check all the time and then you will always be right.

17. Sad to say, many words break this rule, but we will easily find clues for those words, e.g. rapid.
18. Now complete teacher's page 6 by crossing off one of the numbers in Safety and one of the numbers in Danger. Check if the numbers of page 6 match with page 7.
19. Homework: Add a few words to each page in your Decoding Book.

Final Question: WHAT DID YOU LEARN ON THESE TWO PAGES?

> Suggestion: Do not include exceptions in this first session activity.

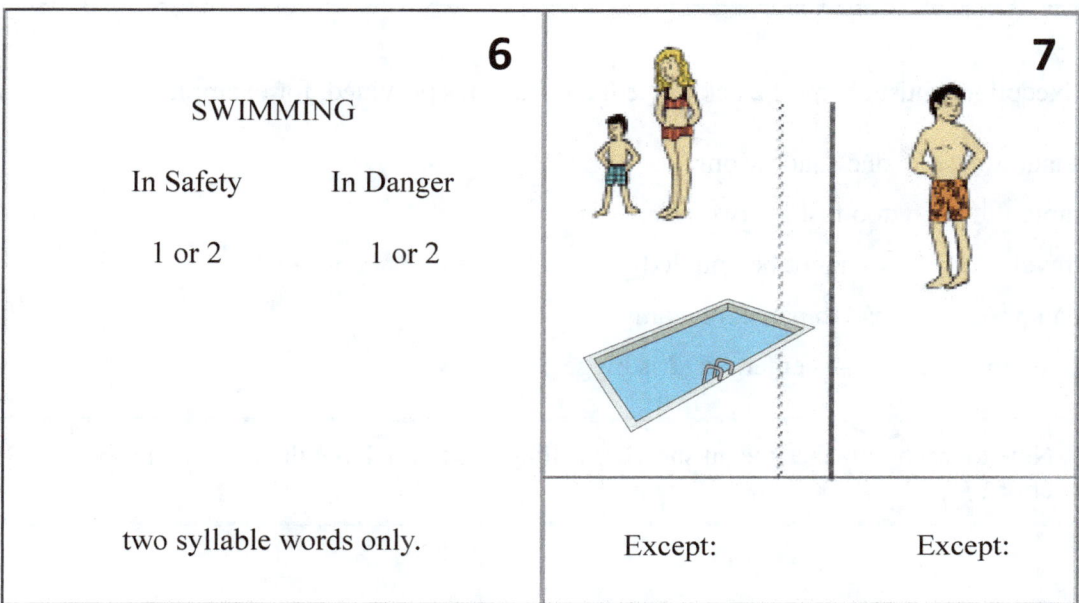

If in danger the vowel says it name

IN SAFETY

two

happy	dinner	running	tidy	taper	hiding
penny	supper	hopping	pony	later	mining
puppy	ladder	tapping	baby	cater	fuming
fluffy	hammer	missing	fury	paper	waving
funny	nipper	filling	roly	liner	taping
mummy	gutter	getting	poly	miner	sloping
daddy	summer	milling	lazy	piper	groping
yummy	better	shopping	tiny	tuna	sliding
hurry	dipper	spinning	wiry	wiper	shaping
poppy	runner	stepping	shady	spider	shining
floppy	fitter	flapping	tony	whiner	whining
tinny	potter	dressing	hazy	sniper	grating
sorry	clatter	padding	story	shaver	shaving
carry	flipper	trotting	shiny	tunic	chasing
spotty	butter	snapping	wavy	milo	gaping
puppet	thinner	pressing	spiny	faded	paving
sudden	slipper	fretting	crazy	fated	slaving
happen	spinner	chipping	wily	writer	writing
flatten	stepper	flipping	diner	dining	
written	splutter	lady	finer	hoping	

IN DANGER

one

Part 2: Decoding Words   41

Exceptions

Exceptions must always be acknowledged and clues provided, for example:

shadow	one shadow only
rapid	too fast for two p's
travel	v cannot be doubled
panic	bad to panic, one only
swollen	means enlarged (2 is bigger)

> Note to teacher: Is the student showing willingness to think out things, making an effort?

Activity 8: When Cat 'C' Changes His Sound

Aim: To develop further thinking strategies when visualising letter c followed by e, i and y.

Preparation: Three pictures for pages 8 and 9 (See Appendix 6), scissors, glue, Students Decoding Book, ruler, pens.

Procedure:

1. Teacher copies teacher's page 8 into Decoding Book or onto board.
2. Student cuts out three pictures and makes 3 sections on page 9.
3. Page 45: the teacher's page 8 should show: .....

    does not like

    ....

    Agree that this is not very helpful, so look at the pictures to find the solution.
4. Directed to the student - What are the pictures? Cent, city, cycle on a bicycle, and what do you notice about the first sound in the words – /s/ - cent, /s/ - city, /s/ - cycle?
5. /Ssss/? Good. So, on the page, is the margin going to come first or last?
6. In the margin, write the sound you hear at the beginning of each picture.
7. Good. Lock up /s/ in each section.
8. First section. Beside the 'cent', write 'cent' (money). (At first the student will write 'sent'.) Ah, why can't you use the 's' here? What letter could you substitute for the 's'? No idea? Well write the words 'ice', 'rice', 'race'. What did you use instead of 's'? (If student is still puzzled teacher could writes, 'ss', 'se', and 'ce' in a column.) Now can you pick which /s/ would be right for cent? Good, it's a bossy e, annoying the cat c and making it to say sss!! Now you know that sometimes 'c' says /s/.
9. (With another student 'cent' will be correct at the very beginning, pointing to the 'c'.) That says /k/ doesn't it? Why?

    Does it say /s/ here? Let's look back at Activity 5 [Page 32] of your Decoding Book. What does that tell you about 'e'? Good, it's Bossy e. Now go back to Activity 8 [Page 9] in of your Decoding Book: 'c – e'.
10. Let's write some words from the 'ce' list.
11. Second section: write 'city' (this is usually correct). Why does 'c' say /s/ here?
12. (Refer to Activity 6, margin letters.) Look, e = y, i = y, they help each other, so would they be friends?
13. 'C' does not like Bossy e so is not friends with 'i' or 'y' either, and again says the /s/ sound.

14. Let us write some words from the 'ci' list.
15. (Refer margin letters in Activity 6, locked ups.) Write in the substitute letters in the first two sections, the letters you use instead of locked up 's'.
16. Students usually write 'c' by itself. Fun discussion – 'C' says /s/-does it? Doesn't it say /k/ there? Make 'c' say 's' in both sections: 'ce' and 'ci'. In the third section, what other letter would boss 'c'?
17. (Students write 'cy' in the margin, remembering third friend 'y' in Activity 6.)
18. Write 'cycle'. Up in the corner of the section write 'bi = 2', then write 'bicycle', and one or two other words from list.
19. Now complete teacher's page. Very good.
20. Homework; cut out ten separate pictures for next activity pages 11 & 12 (see Templates in Appendix 6).

Final Question: WHAT DID YOU LEARN ON THESE TWO PAGES?

TEACHER'S PAGE | STUDENT'S PAGE

——— does not like ———— —	8	Ⓢ	[20 cent coin]	9
——— does not like ———— —		Ⓢ	[city skyline] City; end in y
——— does not like ———— —		Ⓢ	[girl on bicycle] to Cycle on a bicycle

C does not like 'bossy' e, 'bossy' i, 'bossy' y.

cc	cent	cedar	celery	celebrity
	cell	cement	cereal	centenary
	ice	censor	century	ceremony
	vice	celtic	ceramic	certificate
	rice	central	centigrade	accelerate
	price	centric	centipede	intercede
	dice	cellar	celebrate	intercept
	mice	except	licorice	interlace
	race	accept	certify	hyphenated
	grace	finance	certitude	extravagance
	trace	licence	intercede	benevolence
	pace	parcel	indices	magnificence
	place	defence	residence	
	space	pretence	diligence	
	brace	advance	pretence	
	dance	enhance	introduce	
	glance	distance	observance	
	chance	entrance	maintenance	
	mince		penitence	

Part 2: Decoding Words

ci	city	facing	citizen	accidental
	civil	racing	cicada	society
	cider	forcing	accident	pacifier
	cinder	fencing	pacific	precipitate
	cigar	pencil	pacifism	participate
	circus	council	pacify	emancipate
	docile	explicit	exercise	
cy	cyst	lacy	legacy	emergency
	cycle	fancy	bicycle	permanency
	cyclone	mercy	infancy	tendency
	cygnet	pricy	policy	frequency
	cylinder	spicy	potency	decency

Note to tutor: Help student to sort words from their school spelling list. There should be evidence of improvement in school spelling tests now, if not before.

Activity 8.b: 'c' or 'k' to Start a Word

Aim: To develop Thinking Strategies when using 'c' or 'k' at the beginning of words.

Preparation: Ten pictures form pages 11 and 12 (see Templates in Appendix 6), scissors, glue, Students Decoding Book, ruler, pens.

Procedure:

1. Cut out pictures, ask what is the common sound, i.e c or is it k?
2. Revise previous patton (activity 8), i.e when c followed by bossy i or y, the c says ssss. Separate pictures that repeat that patton.
3. If these words cannot start with a c, what can we use – k.
4. Do we use c or k for the remainder words – c.
5. Look at the sound at the beginning of words, what side of the page do we rule margins?
6. On page 10, rule sections across the page for c, ci, and cy ???????
7. Referring back to page 9 and remembering cat 'c' does not like Bossy e, i, or y.
8. Directed to student – Choose any picture, try busy 'c' first.
9. Does cat 'c' like the letter next to it? What does cat 'c' not like? (These two questions should be asked for every picture).
10. Place chosen picture on the correct page in any section.
11. Directed to teacher – Tutor does not need to direct placing of pictures as student will realise any mistakes later.
12. Repeat procedure until all pictures are placed.
13. Each margin 'k' or 'c' needs a letter to follow to match the sound next to the 'k' or 'c' in the picture, e.g. 'cr' for crown, necessitating some changes to picture placement by student.
14. When all letters and pictures have been placed correctly, do we put them at the beginning, or at the end of the line? Glue the pictures in.
15. Student will find a clear message by looking at these two pages. Discuss the value of the message. Think up words.
16. Practise words from lists, either orally, responding quickly by pointing to pages, or by writing words in correct sections.
17. Homework: revise and write words.

Final Question: WHAT DID YOU LEARN ON THESE TWO PAGES?

TEACHER'S PAGE

10

C or K

at the beginning of words or syllables?

When a **c** sound at the beginning of a word is followed by **a**, **e**, **i**, or **y**, it will be a **k** (for kitten). If not, it will be a c (for cat).

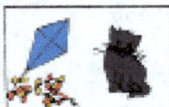

STUDENT'S PAGE

11

'C' or 'K' at the beginning of words or syllables?

ke	ken	kelpy	kebab	ca	cab	cabin	calico
	keg	ketch	sketches		came	cactus	cabinet
	kelp	kettle	sketching		card	camper	canister
	kelt	kennel	sketchers		cash	carpet	cardigan
	ketch	ketchup	kestrels		cave	carrot	calendar
	keep	keeper	sketchily	co	cob	comet	coconut
	kept	keeping	skeleton		code	comic	co-edit
	keen	keenness	kerosene		cold	cobra	costliest
	keel	ketches	kedgeree		colt	cobweb	cosmetic
	kerb	kernel	kerbstone		cost	costume	corrugated
ki	kid	kidnap	kinship	cu	cutlet	cup	cultivate
	kin	kipper	kipper		cubic	cube	cucumber
	kiln	killer	kitbags		cupid	cult	cultural
	kilo	kilted	kindnesses		culprit	cut	culminate
	kilt	kindly	kindlier		curry	cubs	customer
	kind	kindle	kindling	cl	clever	club	clippety
	kite	kismet	kilogram		climax	clip	clarinet
	kitty	kindred	kilotonnes		clinic	clamp	classify
	skin	skillet	kilovolt		clover	clump	clustering
	skim	skinny	kimono		clumsy	clinch	
	skip	skivvy	kitchen	cr	crumpet	crab	criminal
	skid	skipper	pumpkin		credit	crop	crocuses
	skit	kingdom	mankind		crashes	crust	critical
	skimp	kingpin	bumpkin		crisis	crisp	crocodile
					create	cram	crediting

Part 2: Decoding Words

Activity 9: /C/ or /K/ to Finish a Word

Aim: To develop Thinking Strategies when using /k/ sound at the end of short words or syllables.

Preparation: Three pictures for pages 12 and 13 (See Appendix 6), scissors, glue, Students Decoding Book, ruler, pens, Safe & Danger chart.

Procedure:

1. Teacher copies teacher's page 12 into the Decoding Book or onto board.
2. Student cuts out pictures, rules Safe & Danger lines in Decoding Book the same as Students Page 13 below.
3. Together read Teacher's heading page 12.
4. Directed to student – What are the pictures? Mother cat, two kittens.
5. One kitten runs away. Will he be safe alone? No. So where will you put him if he's in danger? Good. Danger side.
6. What about kitten with mother cat? Is he safe with his mother? Yes? So where will you put them? Good. Safe side.
7. Refer to page twelve Teacher's heading. In these words, where is the catch sound going to be? Yes, at the end.
8. Where will you put the pictures, at the beginning of the line, or the end of the line? Good, the end. Now glue them in.
9. Using red or green pen, write 'c' or 'k' on the appropriate pictures, in the correct colours.
10. Should you leave the kitten alone? Is he in danger? What is the last letter of danger words? Yes 'e'. So in danger, which letter could look after kitten, 'k'? Good, 'e', 'ke'.
11. Now write 'ck', 'ke' at the top.
12. Do you have your Safe & Danger chart, green pen, red pen?
13. We are ready for words. First word is 'back'.

    /a/ which picture? (chart)

    green or red? (pen)

    safe or danger? (column)

Directed to teacher – Teacher repeats 'back'. Sometimes a helpful question is: "Is the kitten with his mother or by himself?" Talk To Pencil: 'back'.

14. Using the same procedure, practise words from lists.
15. Extension – Two syllable words from lists.
16. Complete Teacher's page and discuss kitten 'k' not alone. Well done. Homework.

Final Question: WHAT DID YOU LEARN ON THESE TWO PAGES?

Notes:	School Spelling: Teacher helps sort out the words by their patterns. Use Decoding Book categories, or clues e.g. in Building Spelling Cleverness (Part 4.)
	Year 4 and younger children may stop work on the Decoding Book at this point, if the teacher judges it appropriate.

TEACHER'S PAGE

12

---------------- or ----------------

at the end of

short words or syllables?

is

mostly NOT alone

STUDENT'S PAGE

13

'K' sound at the end of short words and syllables

In Safety					In Danger				
rack	lack	sack	pack	slack	rake	sake	lake	make	brake
back	jack	hack	tack	black	fake	bake	cake	take	stake
deck	heck	neck	peck	check	peke				
speck	fleck	wreck							
tick	sick	lick	pick	stick	like	bike	mike	hike	spike
nick	rick	wick	kick	prick	alike	strike			
dock	lock	pock	mock	cock	poke	coke	joke	woke	stroke
rock	sock	tock	clock	stock	yoke	stoke	bloke	choke	broke
tuck	buck	suck	duck	luck	duke				
pluck	truck	chuck	ruck	sack					

Part 2: Decoding Words

Two Syllables

pocket	ticket	taken	choking
cricket	wicket	baker	stoking
chicken	wicked	hiker	stroking
bucket	picket	broken	biking
blacken	reckon	shaker	striking
pucker	locking	maker	joking
stocking	sucking	poker	poking
tucking	kicking	striker	flaking
ducking	flocking	stoker	provoking
packing	reckless	broker	

> Note to Teacher: Student should be confident many things by now, but especially with new challenges that you are offering.

Activity 10: K Needs One [consonant] Friend Only

Aim: To further develop reasoning when /k/ sound has one friend only.

Preparation: Five pictures for page 15 (See Appendix 6), scissors, glue, Students Decoding Book, ruler, pens.

Procedure:

1. Teacher copies Teacher Page 14 into Decoding Book or onto board.
2. Student cuts out pictures, notices /k/ sound at end.
3. Together they read Teacher's Heading and look at pictures.
4. Directed to student – Where is /k/ sound in the words? So, where will the margin be? Good, at the end of the lines.
5. Draw the margin.
6. How many pictures? How many divisions? Yes, 5. Draw the lines.
7. Where do you place the pictures? – Good, near the margin.
8. Let's say the pictures again. What sound comes last? Good, /k/.
9. Listen: /desk/, say 'desk'. What sound comes before /k/? Good. /s/.
10. On the teacher's page, under the word only write 's'.
11. Directed to the teacher – For each picture repeat the procedure and write the appropriate letters underneath in a column.
12. Leave the word 'hawk' until the last.
13. Directed to the student. Using scrap paper write the word 'saw'.
14. Underline the two letters that say /aw/ in /saw/. Hawk has /aw/ in the middle and the clue for 'hawk' is 'saw'. (I saw a hawk).
15. Now write 'hawk'. Which letter comes before /k/ in 'hawk'? Add w to the list on page 14 of your Decoding Book.
16. Now you have all the sounds that come before the /k/ and these sounds could have /k/ to follow in words you do not know at all.
17. What are you going to do about this /k/? Which? 'k' or 'c'? You are not too sure? Well,…
18. Suppose you write both 'c' and 'k' beside each letter, all the way down.
19. Does that look right? No?
20. Suppose you pretend these three letters are three friends in the back seat of a car, s – c – k.
21. Would you like to be squashed in the middle? No?

22. Well, out goes the middle letter! So, cross out cat /c/ all the way down, and which /k/ are you left with? That is it.
23. On page 15 in the margin write the friend, and 'k', in each section. Notice the friend takes the place of cat /c/.
24. Practise saying /sk/, /nk/, /rk/, /lk/ and /wk/, and write the word for each picture.
25. Complete Teacher's page. Well done!
26. For homework, practise writing words from lists.

Final Question: WHAT DID YOU LEARN ON THESE TWO PAGES?

TEACHER'S PAGE

14

A ………………….. connects with 'k' one friend only.

A **c** sound followed by a consonant use **c** for cat.

STUDENT'S PAGE

15

Wink!

A carton of milk

'K' one friend only c/k

ank	bank	sank	tank	rank	blank
	clank	plank	flank	frank	drank
	prank	crank	spank	thank	tanker
ink	pink	wink	link	rink	sink
	blink	clink	drink	slink	think
	shrink	sinker	tinker	drinker	thinker
	blinker	twinkle	crinkle	tinkle	winkle
	sprinkle	sprinkling	shrinking	thinking	trinket
onk	honk	plonk			
unk	bunk	dunk	hunk	junk	punk
	sunk	chunk	clunk	drunk	flunk
	spunk	trunk	shrunk	debunk	shrunken
rk	ark	park	mark	dark	bark
	hark	lark	shark	spark	stark
	darken	darker	darkly	marker	market
	parkas	sparkle	sparkly	cork	fork
	pork	work	stork	corking	snorkel
sk	ask	bask	mask	task	basket
	casket	desk	risk	disk	brisk
	whisk	whisky	risky	frisk	frisky
	dusk	husky	rusk	musket	tusk
	musk	dusky			
lk	milk	silk	whelk	walk	talk
	chalk	folk	yolk	bulk	sulk
wk	hawk	awkward			

Part 2: Decoding Words   55

Activity 11: C Needs One Friend Only

Aim: To further develop reasoning when /k/ sound has only one friend.

Preparation: (For two pages) 17 and 19, three pictures (See Appendix 6), scissors, glue, Students Decoding Book, ruler, pens.

Procedure:

1. Teacher copies two Teacher's pages 16 and 18, into Decoding Book or onto board.
2. Student cuts out pictures, notices /k/ sounds.
3. Directed to student – page 17. How many pictures? How many sections? 2.
4. Rule larger section for picture of picture.
5. Notice position of /k/ sounds – (centre). Where will you place these? Correct, in the centre.
6. Page 17, start to write the word picture, /p - i…
7. Next sound? /k/ Good-which /k/? Let us put both 'c' and 'k' under the word 'only' on page 16.
8. After 'ck'? 't'. So, after 'ck' write 't'. Three friends again, 'ckt', so which letter goes? Cross out the middle 'k'.

   Three friends sitting in the back seat of a car. Their names were c, k and t. It gets rather squishy and tight with three in the back seat. Who is the best to leave so the other two can have more room? Take out the middle figure, K.

9. Now on page 17 finish the word 'picture': /ct – u – re/ (spoken clearly).
10. Practise words from list, extending some – act, actor, active.
11. Now, the 'picnic' picture, start to write, /p - i…/
12. The next sound is /k/-which /k/ sound? Let us put both 'c' and 'k' under the letters ckt on page 16.
13. Next sound? /n/ - ckn. Three friends again, 'ckn', so which letter goes? Cross 'k' out.
14. (Interrupt here for activity on pages 18 and 19 [can 'c' finish alone]. Then…)
15. Now finish picnic.
16. Complete Teacher's page 16 and follow on to extension exercise.

A consonant followed by a c can be can be friends. A consonant is C's friend only.

'K' sound, one friend only

act	act	fact	tact	pact	tract
	enact	exact	react	impact	intact
	enacted	exacted	reacted	reactor	tractor
	acted	actor	impacted	tactful	factor
	factory	protractor	protracted	activate	arctic
	benefactor	practical	practice	practise	retract
ect	elect	reject	detect	protect	inject
	neglect	rejection	detective	protection	injected
	elective	electricity	plectrum	injection	electric
ict	victim	victor	dictum	victory	friction
	evicted	dictate	picture	pictorial	juncture
	dictionary	puncture	picturesque	dictator	junction
oct	doctor	proctor	concoct	doctorate	october
	indoctrinate	octopus	nocturnal	octave	octagon
cn	picnic				

Part 2: Decoding Words

Activity 11b: Can C Finish Alone

Aim: To continue reasoning for /k/ sound at end of longer 'ic' words.
Preparation: Already completed.
Procedure:

1. Page 19, how many pictures? How many sections? 1.
2. (Together read page 18.) Where do you place the picture? At the very end.
3. Teacher and student read Teacher's page 18 again.
4. Directed to student – Which /k/ is going to be alone at the end of longer 'ick' words?
5. (Discuss – Kitten going a long way, etc. alone.)
6. (Refer to Activity 9, page 12.) What do we learn about kitten /k/ here? Yes: kitten /k/ mostly not alone.
7. Which is better able to go a long way, a cat or a kitten?
8. Now on page 18, fill in the correct /k/. Yes, cat 'c'.
9. Let us practise Talk To Pencil long words from the list.
10. Finish with 'picnic' and 'fantastic'.
11. Complete Teacher's page 18: /ic/ words.
12. Return to page 17.

Final Question: WHAT DID YOU LEARN ON THESE TWO PAGES?

____ alone at the end of longer ____ words.

'C' alone at the end of longer 'ic' words

comic	basic	cubic	ethic	mimic	music	optic
panic	relic	stoic	tonic	topic	toxic	tunic
epic	antic	attic	colic	arctic	cleric	clinic
cosmic	critic	ethnic	fabric	static	frantic	frolic
garlic						
	gothic	hectic	plastic	peptic	public	rustic
tropic	drastic	logic	magic	civic	topic	tropic
heroic	atomic	erotic	aquatic	botanic	elastic	numeric
organic	domestic	italic	poetic	harmonic	climatic	ironic
magnetic	historic	dramatic	academic	atlantic	fantastic	pacific
artistic	athletic	barbaric	carbolic	catholic	cosmetic	arsenic
cyclonic	dogmatic	anemic	diabetic	ecstatic	systematic	

Activity 12: When G Changes its Sound

Aim: To develop Thinking Strategies when visualising 'g' followed by 'e', 'i' or 'y'.

Preparation: Three pictures for page 21 (See Appendix 6), scissors, glue, Students Decoding Book, ruler and pens.

Procedure:
1. Teacher copies teacher's page 20 into Decoding Book or onto board.
2. Student cuts out the pictures and draws three sections on page 21.
3. Together read page 20, 'Something does not like something'.
4. Directed to student: What pictures have you got? Cage, giant, gym.
5. Listen to 'cage', 'giant' and 'gym'. Can you hear one same sound that comes somewhere in each of these words?
6. Yes? /j/, /j/, /j/. Good. Is it going to matter where you draw the margin? Not really.
7. Now glue in your pictures: cage, giant, gym.
8. In the first margin write the letter for the sound you hear in each of these words.
9. 'j', 'j', 'j', 'Lock up' each of these.
10. In the first section write 'cage'. Not sure? What about age? Fine. Now 'cage' – 'page' and underline the two letters that say /j/.
11. Let us write down a few more words from the list.
12. Can you fix the margin? What did you use instead of the locked up /j/? 'g' Fine, but does that 'g' say /j/ – oh yes, bossy e , now that 'ge' says /j/.
13. Second section. Write giant, a giant ant. Remember, a different section— good. What about magic, margin?
14. Can you fix the margin in this section? What did you use instead of the locked up /j/? 'g'

    Excellent, but does that 'g' say /j/? – oh yes, bossy i, now that 'gi' says /j/.
15. What about the margin of the third section? You have bossy e, bossy i already, what is the bossy letter this time? Of course, bossy y.
16. Write 'gym'.
17. Now complete teacher's page. Excellent.
18. Homework: Ask Mum to give you some more words and next session we may find some words that will break this rule.

Final Question: WHAT DID YOU LEARN ON THESE TWO PAGES?

TEACHER'S PAGE	STUDENT'S PAGE
20	21
____ alone at the end of longer ____ words.	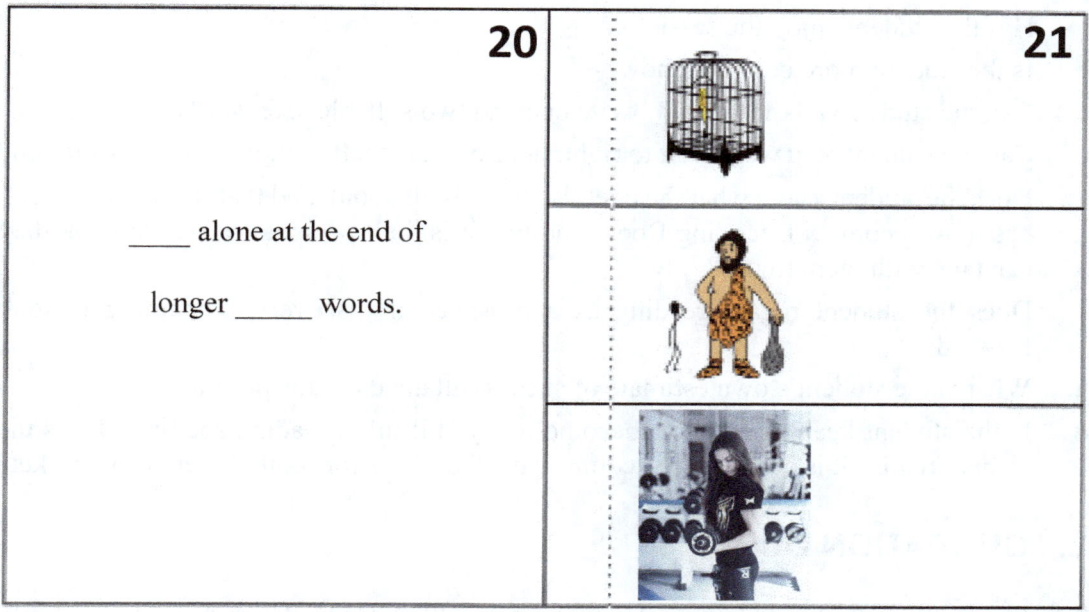

G does not like bossy e, bossy i, or bossy y.

ge	gem	germ	gents	gentle	gender	gently
	gentry	genius	age	cage	gage	rage
	huge	barge	forge	gorge	George	hinge
	change	charge	large	lunge	lounge	plunge
	merge	range	singe	fringe	stage	surge
	twinge	grange	cringe	avenge	damage	deluge
	dosage	emerge	digest	engage	forage	garage
	homage	manage	mirage	oblige	angel	orange
	ravage	refuge	savage	voyage	enlarge	legend
	ginger	regent	pigeon	engage	vengeance	envisage
	bandage	vegetable	infringe	sergeant	magic	energetic
gi	giant	digit	rigid	gipsy	waging	engine
	ginger	logic	paging	raging	gigantic	margin
	tangible	marginal	gibing	singeing		
gy	gym	gyp	gybing			
	mangy	cagy				
	bulgy	orgy	elegy	eulogy		

EXCEPTIONS are numerous:
| | gear | gelding | geese | tigers | augers | gilder |
| | begin | gift | foggy | boggy | given | gilt |

Part 2: Decoding Words 61

1. EVALUATION after completing Parts 1 and 2

a. Has the student enjoy the sessions?
b. Is the student more confident now?
c. Can the student 'talk to pencil', write one and two syllable safe words?
d. Can the student read words left to right, lines of words left to right without hesitation?
e. Does the student know what the exercise book is all about, and that the exercise book has now become a Decoding Book, and that it is their personal reference book they can take with them to use?
f. Does the student regard reading as a prospect of discovery, something to look forward to?
g. What is the student's own estimate of success attained on this program?
h. Is the student keen to go on to become really skillful at reading/spelling? Does the student realise it is a skill to be acquired just like skills for football, tennis or cricket?

2. FOUNDATION LAID

Teacher and student should both feel that a start has been made, the student is on the way and looks forward to the future with confidence and joy. Time for a break: this is necessary to consolidate, to allow what has been learned to become instinctive before the next level of learning is tackled.

Part 3

Discovering Reading Success (pulling it all together)

By the time the student reaches this section, he or she should be quite confident about the way in which words are structured in English. Confidence should be returning, and reading of extended passages may now be introduced. Students should be invited to analyse their own reading, using the 'Twelve Reading Checkpoints' that follow. Future instruction will be based on that analysis.

Discovering Reading Success

Reading Check Points

Most children with reading and spelling difficulties know that their reading is not as good as they wish they could. Once they have some mastery of the spelling patterns of the language, it is time to move on to reading itself. After a time, their own assessment of their needs in reading can be used as a basis for work. Here we have listed common faults in children's reading in the form of questions for them to answer. When the child has answered them, they should be briefly discussed. In this way, the student diagnosis his or her own needs. Most children do not have to answer "no" to more than a couple of questions if they have had substantial language experience through the earlier parts of this program. An understanding of these problems often results in the child being able to eliminate them without much assistance.

1. Am I reading fast enough?

Most remedial children have to answer no to this question, though the child in Fig 5d (p. 10) would be an exception. At worst, the reading may be so slow that the child has forgotten the beginning of the sentence by the time he reaches the end. If that is so, there will probably be other associated problems. If this is the only problem of the twelve, then the child is like the one in Fig 7 (p.11), and the use of an 'eye movement trainer' would be helpful. Such an instrument is a flexible rod about 15–20 cm long and roughly the width of a line of print (6 mm). At first the teacher, and later the child pushes this pointer along the line of print from left to right to control the movement and speed of the eyes, and hence the reading:

Our conversation and hand

A 20 cm garment stiffener or a strip cut from the side of a plastic ice-cream

> **The Twelve Reading Checkpoints**
>
> 1. Am I reading fast enough?
> 2. Am I stopping often enough?
> 3. Am I stopping at the right places?
> 4. Are the first two words after stopping always correct?
> 5. Am I quick at the end of every phrase or sentence?
> 6. Is my brain helping to finish long or difficult words?
> 7. Is my memory supplying frequently repeated words or names?
> 8 (a) Am I reading straight ahead without my eyes checking back?
>   (b) Do my eyes skip words and go too far ahead?
> 9. Am I 'double-reading'? or, am I saying the words to myself before I say them out loud?
> 10. Am I reading the story or only the words?
> 11. Am I thinking about the subject (story) or something else?

container serves the purpose very well. 'Pushing' with the eye movement trainer forces the pace if it is done at the right speed, that is, just faster than the child is vocalizing. The rod 'forces' the eyes to keep moving ahead, and, because it covers the words progressively, makes regressive eye-movements ('checking back') useless. Marked and immediate increase in speed without loss of comprehension may be achieved once the child can push himself. After a time, when the movement has become habitual, the eye-movement controller may be used as a pointer held above the line of print. This allows for further increase in speed:

Very rarely should a child's eyes be 'pulled' along the line (using the rod from the right hand side of the page) as this negates most of the reasons for using the eye movement trainer. The few cases where 'pulling' may be advised are, (a) when the child cannot be persuaded to stop at the ends of phrases, sentences etc. (see under Checkpoints 2,3,4, below); (b) with a child whose eyes persistently jump forward, and regressive eye-movements are not a problem; (c) with a child who is persistently back-to-front and need practice in looking first at the beginning of each word; (d) where a child persistently guesses words and get them wrong, reading, for example, said: for does (here he is reversing the word as well). Teachers need to practise pushing children's reading so that they can adjust to the needs of individual children and see in advance the textual problems to be overcome by the child. This is not easy when one is sitting opposite the child and having to read ahead and upside-down! Study the passage and comments at the end of this section, bearing in mind the other reading checkpoints.

2. Am I Stopping Often Enough?

This question draws attention to the need to phrase the reading according to its meaning, and not just to read 'words'.

3. Am I Stopping at the Right Places?

Figure 5d is an extreme example of a child with this problem, while 5c, 7 and 8 have it in different degrees. The solution is to push the child to the end of each phrase, then stop. Initially, the pause may be quite long (see 4 below).

When the child has read a paragraph well, recorded it, listen to it together, ask him to listen to himself later. Reinforce his own good work. If he persists in "reading on", the teacher may for a while have to "pull" his reading instead of pushing him. Very occasionally, one comes across a child who insists that he is reading well despite the fact that he is reading badly. In extreme cases, it will be necessary to record the bad reading and let him hear it: he probably does not listen to himself at all. This measure is a last resort, to be used only when a child cannot see that there is a deficiency.

4. Are the first two words after stopping always correct?

This is most important. During the pause at the end of a phrase or sentence, the eyes should be reading the beginning of the next phrase. The joining words will be important in understanding the connection between the two phrases or sentences, and hence they must be right. The child in Figure 8 above may have this problem. Encourage him to take as long as he likes at the pause, and explain that listeners will be thinking while he is stopping. Then push forward to the end of the next phrase. If it is read correctly, or almost correctly, ask "Did you see all that?" If the answer is "no", the teacher can explain "Your brain read it", which is the ultimate aim, of course. A common difficulty for children who do not get the first two words right after stopping is the digraph. Many joining words begin with wh, th, sh. Use a scatter-chart to practise these sounds. Emphasise speed of recognition and response, and spend most time getting the mouth ready to say the sound, rather than actually responding with the sound.

5. Am I quick at the end of every phrase or sentence?

This is intended to encourage the use of context clues and visual recognition, rather than reading every word, or every part of longer words. Tell the child to let his mind read the end of the phrase. See the sample passage in the box over page.

6. Is my brain helping to finish long or difficult words?

As with 5 above, understanding the context should allow a long word to be finished when only a portion has actually been read. Thus, in a passage about boats, the word harbour need not be totally sounded: har gives the clue, and the eyes should run over -bour to the next word. In the sample passage below, expedition would not need analysis because of the context (i.e. its place in the phrase, "Chinese Zoological Expedition," and the use of capitals). There are of course, some words that will need more careful scrutiny no matter what the context, e.g. names of people. Teachers should be careful to make such distinctions and to indicate them by the way they use the eye movement controller.

7. Is my memory supplying frequently repeated words or names?

In the passage below, for example, the name Benton should be read quicker at the second occurrence – though a slight pause will still be needed. Expedition should be automatic by the third repetition.

8. (a) Am I reading straight ahead without my eyes checking back?

The aim is to keep the eyes moving, because regressive eye movements are a correlative of poor reading. The child in Figure 5c (p. 9) has this problem. Using the eye movement controller to push helps a great deal, as does awareness of the problem. By the time most of our remedial children are at the reading stage, the problem is that they can read the words but lack confidence to keep going. They think they are certain to have been wrong the first time, and so they look back. Encourage them, at this stage it is best to keep going even if they know they were wrong. So long as the errors are not gross, they are best ignored until the end of the paragraph or page, when the child may find and correct any words he knows he read wrongly.

(b) Do my eyes skip words and go too far ahead?

The extreme case is in figure 5d (p. 10), many children have some difficulty on this point. In severe cases, drag instead of pushing with the eye-movement controller. In the commoner cases, simple awareness of the problem is sufficient to check it. In all cases, careful oral reading, followed by a response to the meaning of the passage (retell the story, give an opinion, make a prediction etc.) is necessary.

9. Am I 'double-reading'? Or am I saying the words to myself before I say them out loud?

This problem is one of excessive subvocalisation, where the child first reads the words to himself and then out loud. The alternate phrasing of the question suggested has been a help to some children in identifying this problem, and, once again we find that their recognition of the problem has made an immediate difference to their reading. Explain that they really knew the word when they saw it first, and nothing was gained by saying it twice. Demonstrate the absurdity of "double-reading" by reading a passage aloud, repeating each word as it is read. A minor variation of the problem is the child who has difficulty in saying the words and so finds it necessary to do the preliminary conscious mental process. This child is in Figure 6 (p. 11). Also included in this group is the stammerer. In both of these cases, teach the child to push himself while reading silently. Check comprehension by discussion. If for some reason reading aloud is required, it may be facilitated by allowing the child to trace over the first letter of problem words with a pencil as he speaks the word. It is important that the tracing begin just prior to vocalization.

10. Am I reading the story, or only the words?

"Only words" is the answer in Figures 7 and possibly 8 (p. 11–12). Such cases often have associated defects (2, 3, and 4, above). Once the problem is thus verbalised, the child should begin to exercise his mind on the story and should begin to read with comprehension. In some cases, careful work will be needed on short extracts, progressively exploring the meaning of each part (paragraph or even sentence) and adding it to understandings already gleaned from the discussion of reading already completed.

11. Am I thinking about the subject (story) or something else?

This is really a variant of checkpoint 10, but the reason behind it will be different. It may also be associated with 12, below. With experience, teachers will find this easy to detect from an awareness of their own interest or otherwise in the child's reading. If the teacher finds his attention wandering, he should ask the child, "Just a moment, what are you thinking about?" He should explain that his own thoughts were wandering, and that the listener always loses interest when the reader loses his involvement in the reading.

12. Am I enjoying reading this story?

If the answer is no, change to another book. A good variety for choice is necessary so that interest will be maintained. When the children have diagnosed their problems by answering yes and no to the questions asked in the twelve reading checkpoints, show them their problem on one of the diagrams, if possible. Then help them to understand and rectify the problem.

Using the Eye-Movement Trainer to Push

When the child is ready to read, that is, when he has had considerable experience in writing words and success in spelling, he should, after an initial trial reading, be encouraged to analyse his own difficulties using the twelve checkpoints above. From then on, he should be encouraged to use the eye-movement controller to help his eyes to move and to increase his speed. With some children, the controller may soon be dispensed with; with others, it will always be necessary when they become tired. For a child with obvious visual problems, the teacher should in the first place use the controller, sitting opposite the child and pushing along the lines of print at a speed just faster than the child is vocalizing. Pause briefly at the beginning of long or difficult words, then push on to the end of the word, slowing slightly to complete the phrase. Stop at the end of the sentence, or wherever a pause is required for the sense. Soon the child should be allowed to push himself. At first he should push along the line, that is, so that the controller covers the words he has read. As facility increases, the controller may be used as a pointer above the line of print to allow greater speed. Pointing below the line will usually be found to slow the reading. It will be found that some children read well with the teacher pushing, but on their own gradually develop lazy habits such as pointing word-by-word or using the pointer below the line. They should always be encouraged to realise what is happening for themselves, and to this end the teacher may simply refrain from commenting on their reading until they become aware of the deterioration themselves. Alternatively, the teacher may take over the pushing from the child, commenting that he is doing so because he can see that the child is getting tired. The difference in performance with the teacher pushing will be noticed by the pupil. Here is a sample passage to illustrate some of the factors to be borne in mind by the teacher. A first-form boy who was having difficulty in reading an interesting passage about spies and ships without the aid of the controller, read this passage perfectly, at sight, once the controller was used as a pointer above the words.

1	Dear Mr. Lewis,
2	It gives me great pleasure to confirm our
3	conversation and hand you this letter of appointment to the
4	Chinese Zoological Expedition under the leadership of Mr. John

5	Benton. The terms of the engagement are as follows:
6	1. The period will be for the duration of the expedition,
7	approximately one year.
8	2. All your expenses will be paid from the time you leave
9	New York until you return. In addition you will receive a
10	salary of two thousand dollars a month.
11	3. You are to join Mr. Benton in China, wherever he
12	directs, by the first ship.
13	4. The object of the expedition is to explore the
14	mountains of southwest China and eastern Tibet for the

Notes on the passage:

Line 2 *pleasure* Some children have difficulty with the endings of longer words, frequently misreading them.

Watch for this, and if apparent, pause with the controller halfway through the word instead of pushing quickly on as usual: pleas/ure

Line 3 *conversa/tion*; 1.4, appoint/ment, etc. (Note the number of words ending in -ion in this passage.)

Line 4 *Chinese Zoological Expedition*. If the child's home is literate and his language background good, he should be able to work through this difficult phrase with ease. What word, other than zoological could begin with zoo? And, in context, what else could follow, beginning with Exp, than Expedition? Encourage the child over and over: "If your head (brain) knows, and you have heard the word, you can read it." If necessary, pause briefly at the beginnings of the words, then push on to the end.

Line 5 *Benton*. Give time for this word, as it will need analysis.

Line 6 *expedition*. Memory should supply it from 1.4, so do not allow too much time.

Line 7 *approximately*. Pause momentarily after approx, then push on to the end of the word. Once approx has been observed, the brain should supply the rest.

Line 11 Benton. Pause briefly. Memory should help, but it is not a common name like Brown. *wherever*. Pause at the r. The word could be *whenever* if not carefully observed. If the child has problems with wh, refer to the chart for mouthing wh, th, ch, sh. Practise, so that the mouth gets ready to say it before the word is begun.

Line 13 expedition. On its third occurrence, this should be read without pause. Ends of lines: move the controller quickly to the beginnings of new lines, especially when a line ends in a word such as a (1.9), the (1.13), or he (1.11).

Part 4 and the Sound Dictionary

Part 4 and Jenny's Sound Dictionary (Section 2) will be a different and more advanced challenge, building onto the skills already mastered.

The next sections teach the student how to remember catchy words without memorising, compile a dictionary of words grouped by sounds, and discover where certain syllables belong, and to which category they belong. It is virtually detective work from observed clues or associated ideas. The words come from school-based lists. This study actually involves reading and will lead easily into consideration of the skills required in reading.

Part 4

Building Spelling Cleverness

This part contains the following sections to assist with studying spelling lists:

Word Categories for studying spelling lists

Clues for Catchy Words

- what; was, wash, water; saw; put, push, pull; because; beautiful; sure; to, two, too.

- of; off; he, her, here, where, there; the, there; they, with, witch, which, whether, when; we, were, went, weather.

- how, who, who's, whose; hole, whole; many, any; said, again; one.

- shoe, shoes, does, goes, toes; could, would, should; come, some, love.

- for, from, ever, every, very; are; all.

Word Structure and Finding Links

This part of the Lamond Method deals with short words – CATCHY, because the sounds have no set pattern; they are words with great irregularities. These words appear in early school vocabulary and are in constant use.

Students who have a problem with recalling letter sequences visually, must pick out a few familiar and easy letter combinations (e.g. as in watch – look *at* your watch) on which to build up the word. Students can learn to find these links for themselves once a start is made in the procedure. Here, however, you will find ready-made links or clues.

As this whole method is creative and alive, better links may be hiding, waiting to be found. Have the 'fun' of finding more links! Let the students be in the game, and further their skills. The object is to get children into the habit of observing the structure of words. Children with difficulties in reading and spelling do not do this naturally.

Word Categories for Studying Spelling Lists

The following are mnemonic and analytical clues to help children write and remember the features of English orthography. See which category helps most with any word.

CATEGORY		EXAMPLES
'Talk to pencil' .... words		intend
'Safe' (short vowel) .... words		plan, stop
'Danger' (long vowel) .... words	*v - c+e*	slope
Ending (sound) **e** or **i** .... words	*y*	pony, fly
'Swimming Pool' .... words		dinner, diner
Tricky **s** sound .... words	*c - e/i/y*	cent, ice
Careful **k** sound .... words	*ch k-e*	clock, kite
'<u>a</u>nd I' .... words	*ai*	train, said
'<u>a</u>nd <u>I</u> run' .... words	*air*	stair
<u>are</u> .... words	*are*	fare
h looks like a 'chair' .... words	*h*	vehicle, school
'<u>au</u>nty & uncle' .... words	*au*	laundry
'<u>au</u>nty & <u>u</u>ncle <u>g</u>o <u>h</u>ome .... words	*augh*	daughter
'eat' .... words	*ea*	meat, bread
'see tree' .... words	*ee*	speed
'ear' .... words	*ear*	heard
'I go high' .... words	*igh*	light, tight
'oh a....!' .... words	*oa*	boat
'oh you' .... words	*ou*	cousin, country
'<u>oh</u> <u>you</u> <u>r</u>un' .... words	*our*	journey, court
'<u>oh</u> <u>you</u> <u>g</u>o <u>h</u>ome' .... words	*ough*	enough

Clues For Catchy Words

what
Write 'hat'	hat
Teacher asks 'what hat'?	what
Answer "the hat with **W** in front"	

was, wash, water, etc.
Write as, put a letter to start for was, wash...	was, wash
Write at, add letters to make water, watch	water, watch
Clue … as I was … as I wash	wash
water at the tap	water
look at your watch	water
I want an ant	want

saw
Link word; scratchy claw, (w) for saw	saw
Clue … I saw a claw.	claw

U = container
Write U on four separate lines	*pu* t
add missing letters for words	*pu* sh
put (in) push (down into) pull (out)	*pu* ll
full (fill it)	*fu* ll

because
'because' is an Aunty and Uncle word	because
Because Aunty and Uncle were coming to visit, bossy Mum (e) said "tidy up"	

beautiful
Dress up … be Aunty and Uncle	beautiful
BEAU tiful, beautiful	
or, BE A **beaut**, Mum …	
Remember, longer word, one l	

sure
The sun for sure	sure

to, two, too
to … on the way to…	to
two … 2 v/s for counting: w = vv	two
too … not quite right … it's too … also	too

of, off
of … a part of…a piece of …	of
off … 2 hands to take something off. 2 feet to walk off	off

he, her, here, where. there
1. Write he five times on separate lines
2. Make he say her   he, her
3. Make he say her to here   here
4. Make he say her to here to where (W =looking up and down)   where
5. Make he say her to here to there (pointing with the t)   there

the, their
Write two words … the bird   the
Put an empty circle after the: **O**
Circle the ir in bird
Now write their bird   th ei r

the, they
Write the … add a letter …   the
the to they   they

with, witch, which, whether, when
One chair (the letter h) with you (to the party)
Write 'with' (only one h)   with
Use wit … write witch, *ch*ase her   witch
Write which, a choice (two h's)   which
Write whether, a choice (two h's)   whether
Write when: is the hen to sit on the chair?   when

we, were, went, weather
Write we, (extend) we to were   we, were
Write we, (extend) we to went   went
Write we, cover the W and make weat, remove your finger
and finish the word … weather   weather
Clue … we eat in all kinds of …

how, who, who's, whose
Write how   how
1. how about the W for who?   who
    who … take the W from the end of how
    how put W at the beginning of who
    who how to who
2. Write who is, shorten who is to who's (notice apostrophe   who's
   for the missing letter)
3. The boss (e) says … 'whose pencil?'
write whose.   whose

hole, whole
Punch a hole in a scrap of paper.
Write hole beside the hole   hole

Oh! I don't want the hole.
Put a patch over the hole, ☐
What is a good letter to darn over the hole? W! whole
Now the hole is whole again.

many, any
Write man, and make man, many many
Write an, and make an, any. any

said, again
And I (ai) words
Using clue, and I (ai) on two separate lines said
make the words said, and again. again

one
Write on and boss on for one on
Write one seven times on separate lines one
You have done one (job) 1st word done
he has done none 2nd word none
and he has gone 3rd word gone
and you are alone 4th word alone
now fit a big C after on for onCe 5th word once
then a letter to start and finish, for honey honey
and a letter to start and finish, for money money
one jar of honey
one piece of money

shoe, shoes, does, goes, toes
Shoo. Write what you hear, shoo
(your shoes) you lose one, so lose an o
Bossy e comes, says "find the shoe"
Now write shoe, add s for shoes shoe
Circle oes in shoes shoes
Using oes, listen for one letter does
Write does, shoes, goes, toes goes
Remember … "He does up his shoes and toes
he goes on his toes".

could, would, should
For Infants children
Going to the Dog
Round the ball o
Over the hole   u
Down the pole i
to the dog   dog ould

Cat travels   • round the ball   0   co
                     • over the hole u   cou
                     • down the pole   1 to the Dog could
Wombat travels   • repeat procedure   would
Sheep travels   • repeat procedure   should

For Primary Children
"Talking to the Dog"
"Oh yoU Little Dog"   OULD

Cat could say "oh you little dog"	could
Worm would say "oh you little dog"	would
Sheep should say "oh you little dog"	should

come, some

Clue 'home'	home
Write come, some	come
	some

love
Listen: "Put an O in "love," says bossy e   love

for, from, ever, every, very
(TALK TO PENCIL)

for from	for from
ever to every	ever
	every
every to very	very
clever and never	clever
	never

are
Write what you hear in 'ar' … two sounds   are
Bossy e says: "Where are you?"

all

Write 'all' on four separate lines	all
	all (etc)
tall	tall
hall	hall
wall	wall
call	call

Leave a space, write the words again, a second time.
Now change the last 'l' in each word to a 'k' so that you have:

	talk
	halt
	walk
	calf

salt is an 'all' word, write salt	salt
half is an 'all' word, write half	half
palm and calm can be 'all' words,	palm
but the second 'L' falls and bends for 'm'	calm

Clues   All need salt, all not half
        All is calm, <u>all</u> teachers used chalk   chalk

'all' at the beginning of words
The joined on word takes the place of the second 'L'
almost, always, altogether

almost
always
altogether

REMEMBER   short words – two 'L's'
longer words one 'L', add more to a longer word, = again two 'L's'.

Extension Exercise:

1. Extend 'picnic' to say 'picnic-ing'.
2. Refer student to page 9 while teacher circles 'ci' and asks "Did you write picnicking, or something else"?
3. Something else – 'picnising'.
4. Which letters should not be together for /k/ sound?
5. How will you separate those two letters 'c – i'?
6. Leave student to discover the answer. Well done!

Final Question: WHAT DID YOU LEARN ON THESE TWO PAGES?

Section 2

Jenny's Sound Dictionary

Index to the Sound Dictionary

(green)

Sound Group	Sound Group no.	Page no.
a e i o u oo	1	(97)
	3	(100)
	5	(104)
	7	(106)
	9	(109)
	11	(111)

(red)

Sound Group	Sound Group no.	Page no.
a e i o u oo	2	(98)
	4	(101)
	6	(105)
	8	(107)
	10	(110)
	12	(112)

Sound Group	Sound Group no.	Page no.	Sound Group	Sound Group no.	Page no.
ow	13	(113)	ch	30	(136)
oy	14	(114)	t	31	(136)
r	15	(115)	z	32	(137)
ar	16	(116)	zh	33	(138)
er	17	(117)	y	34	(139)
air	18	(119)	w	35	(139)
eer	19	(120)	m	36	(140)
or	20	(121)	n	37	(141)
k	21	(122)	ng	38	(143)
s	22	(125)	d	39	(144)
g	23	(127)	b	40	(145)
j	24	(128)	p	41	(145)
l	25	(129)	h	42	(145)
f	26	(131)	Letter-Based Groups		
v	27	(132)	(Same letters-different sounds)		(146)
th	28	(133)	ough		
sh	29	(134)	augh		
			our		
			x		
			Irregular Words		(147)

The index page for the Sound Dictionary. Colour the box in the left hand column green (safe short) and in the right hand column red (danger, long) to assist in differentiating the long and short vowel sounds.

The Sound Dictionary: Building Word Families

Having dealt with some irregular words in the section 'Building Spelling Cleverness' we now move on to irregular word patterns, e.g. train, eat, light, mention, etc.

If the words are dealt with systematically, as they emerge from Year 1, the youngsters can enjoy acquiring skills in observation and reasoning instead of 'learn' or 'remember by rote' methods, which require series of unreasonable letter sequences being held in memory.

In the Decoding Book Sound Dictionary, the child builds up families of words according to their sounds. Each sound of the language is grouped on one (or more) pages of the dictionary, and the pages are divided into sections for the various spellings of that sound. The spellings are printed in the outer margin of the page. Because this book is compiled progressively, a loose leaf format can sometimes be found useful. The analysis of the sounds and spellings of the language is given in Fig. 1, p. 7

Additional pages deal with tricky words in 'Silly Sentences' or other mnemonic devices, and here sound may not be so important as spelling (e.g. Letter-Based Groups, p. 149, where all the 'ough' words regardless of sound are collected. There is no way the letters 'ough' can be sounded out.) The Sound Dictionary is a special book, preferably a small loose leaf folder because pages can be inserted out of their number sequence as they are required. This very special book becomes a personal dictionary of words collected and arranged by sounds. It also has an 'association of ideas' base, which is helpful for your memory.

Preparation – Your 'Listen – Look – Highlight' Resource Material

1. Take the index and glue this inside the cardboard cover of your new folder.
2. Colour the vowels in the index green for the 'safe' column, red for the 'danger' one.
3. The first page should be the 'listen – look – highlight' sheet opposite the index.
4. Turn this over, put a sample page for ruling the grids next (on right).
5. Then follow the student's work sheet (probably A4 sheets turned so that the margin appears on the outer right hand side of the page).
6. Turn the blank worksheet over and have a supply of Sound Dictionary pictures at the back of the folder ready for use, and easy to find.

Using The Sound Dictionary

Work may begin at any time once the Decoding Book is begun, though in general teachers will prefer to complete the Decoding Book first (see Plan of Work p. 28–29). Early work in the Sound Dictionary consists of 'putting away' words as they are encountered. This means that the child has to analyse words according to their sounds, examine the spelling of these sounds, find the matching spelling in the margin of the appropriate page of the Sound Dictionary, and write the word correctly. Where appropriate, a picture is used to illustrate a 'clue word' for each family, that is, a simple word that gives the clue to the spellings of the whole group. Thus, eat is the clue word for the ea words like meat, seat, etc. Each word family is preceded by an underlined clue word.

When the Decoding Book is complete, work concentrates on the Sound Dictionary, for as long as interest is maintained. Irregular words are selected from the child's school spelling list for the week, and these are 'put away' in the appropriate place. As time permits, other words that are spelt according to the same pattern are written with them. The use of the school spelling list is important, as it relates the remedial work to the "real" work of the classroom. It is there that the child measures his success, rather than during the activity. More than any amount of encouragement from the teacher, success in the normal class situation is what changes a child's attitude to himself, his work, and the world around him.

An example: The word light – we want to 'put light away'

1. The student refers to the page 'Listen – Look', etc.
2. Listen to the word 'light' l-ight. Which sound might have the catch – 'l I gh-t'?
3. Look at the word 'light'. Where is the catch? Yes! /I/
4. How many letters say /I/? Yes, three.
5. Index – which sound are we looking for? Yes, I. Safe or Danger? Yes, danger. Which page? Yes, Sound Group 6.
6. Now make a p. 6. Using sample page mark spots on p. 6. Draw the lines.

Teacher: referring to Sound Dictionary finds 'I' and selects some or all letter combinations and helps the student fill them in, in margin.

1. Find p. 7 pictures. Cut out those required.
2. Then proceed to detective game. Teacher gives clues, e.g."I go high for light".
   A danger word for line, etc.
3. Write words, where teacher suggests.
4. Homework – more words.

Spelling

School spelling lists, if not already backed by the teacher, should be introduced at this point. In the Decoding Book some basic support is available also in 'Clues for Catchy Words'.

As teachers become familiar with this approach to spelling, they will realise that the overall aim is to ensure accuracy at all times so that the student may gain confidence quickly.

Accuracy is only feasible by attacking new words with a category or clue, while 'talking to pencil'. Thus the student will find the satisfaction of being correct.

Given a list of words to write (not to look at) many will pose no problem. Others will demand some kind of recall from the given support. The resulting score should be good and this will be vastly superior to the heartbreaking low scoring found in the average pre-tests. The challenge to the teacher would be better results and happier students. Again, success leads to more success, a basic thought in this method.

Experiment with 'putting away' high school words: The section indicates the tricky part of the word, and sound groups where the word might be 'put away'.

Word: *RESP IR A TI ON* Number of letters: 11 Number of sounds: 9 1st Catch: ir Sound group: er Sound group: 17	2nd Catch: ti Sound group: sh Sound group: 29	**Word:** *AU DIT OR IUM* Number of letters: 10 Number of sounds: 8 1st Catch: au Sound group: or Sound group: 20 1st Clue: Aunty & Uncle	2nd Catch: or Sound group: or Sound group: 20 2nd Clue Horn
Word: *M EA G RE* Number of letters: 6 Number of sounds: 4 1st Catch: ea Sound group: e Sound group: 4 1st Clue: eat	2nd Catch: re Sound group: er Sound group: 17 2nd Clue: fire	**Word:** *DISREP AI R* Number of letters: 9 Number of sounds: 7 1st Catch: air Sound group: air Sound group: 18 1st Clue: **A**nd **I** **R**un	
Word: *REIMB UR SE* Number of letters: 9 Number of sounds: 7 1st Catch: ur Sound group: er Sound group: 17 1st Clue: purse	2nd Catch: se Sound group: s Sound group: 22 2nd Clue: not plural	**Word:** *VEGET AR IA N* Number of letters: 10 Number of sounds: 9 1st Catch: ar Sound group: air Sound group: 18 1st Clue: Mary is a vegetarian	2nd Catch: i Sound group: e Sound group: 4 2nd Clue: taxi

Word:
OV ER B EAR ING
Number of letters: 11

Number of sounds: 7
1st Catch: ear
Sound group: air
Sound group: 18
1st Clue: sing

Word:
DISA PP EAR AN CE
Number of letters: 13

Number of sounds: 9
1st Catch: pp
Sound group: p
Sound group: 41
1st Clue: lots of people

2nd Catch: ear
Sound group: ear
Sound group: 19
2nd Clue: ear tricky s

Word: *CA SH IE R*
Number of letters: 9

Number of sounds: 4
1st Catch: ier
Sound group: eer
Sound group: 19
1st Clue: I want to be a Cashier

Word:
OCTO G EN AR IAN
Number of letters: 12

Number of sounds: 11
1st Catch: g
Sound group: j
Sound group: 24
1st Clue: tricky g

2nd Catch: ar
Sound group: air
Sound group: 18
2nd Clue: Mary

3rd Catch: ce
Sound group: s
Sound group: 22

3rd Catch: i
Sound group: e
Sound group: 4
3rd Clue: taxi

Word:
AR CH ITE C T URE
Number of letters: 12

Number of sounds: 9
1st Catch: ch
Sound group: k
Sound group: 21
1st Clue: school

2nd Catch: c
Sound group: k
Sound group No 21
2nd Clue: clear speech

Word: *A CQ U IR E*
Number of letters: 7

Number of sounds: 5
1st Catch: cq
Sound group: k
Sound group: 21
1st Clue: cats

2nd Catch: u
Sound group: w
Sound group: 35
2nd Clue: rush everywhere

Word: *FREQ UENT*
Number of letters: 8

Number of sounds: 8
1st Catch: q
Sound group: k
Sound group: 21
1st Clue: queen

Word: *CON QU ER OR*
Number of letters: 9

Number of sounds: 6
1st Catch: n
Sound group: ng
Sound group: 38
1st group: sing

2nd Catch: qu
Sound group: k
Sound group: 21
2nd Clue: queen

3rd Catch: u
Sound group: u
Sound group: 10
3rd Clue: clear speech

2nd Catch: re
Sound group: er
Sound group: 17
2nd Clue: quick

2nd Catch: u
Sound group: w
Sound group: 35
2nd Clue: quick

3rd Catch: or
Sound group: or
Sound group: 20
3rd Clue: horn

Jenny's Sound Dictionary

A Spelling list

This 'scaffolded' (supported) approach to a new list of words demands the student's full attention and is creative, with the teacher participating by challenging the child with clues.

    1st requirement: talk to pencil
    2nd requirement: interpret the clue for the 'catch'

Start with 'talk to pencil' in 'no catch' words

1. Absent   2. Educate   3. Instantly

WORDS

4. REGULAR — work out the 'catch', from the clue
   <u>Listen</u> the <u>car</u> has a regu<u>lar</u> check.

5. DIFFER — careful, swimming pool word
   Extend to
   DIFFERENT — <u>Listen</u> for the clue – the <u>rent</u> is different

6. DIFFERENCE — *differ* to *difference* – there is a difference in his fence

7. IGNORANT — talk to pencil
   <u>Listen</u> an <u>ant</u> isn't ignor<u>ant</u>

8. IGNORANCE — <u>careful</u> no ignor<u>ance</u> at the d<u>ance</u>

9. MEANT — I m<u>ea</u>nt to bring br<u>ea</u>d to <u>eat</u>
   <u>careful</u> of e in meant, an 'eat' word

10. ABSENCE — careful – in the abs<u>ence</u> of a <u>fence</u>
    Busy <u>ence</u> e n c e (alphabet)

11. CONVERSATION — con-ver-sa-tion
    Where's the one 'catch'? sh
    <u>Listen</u> – they sat during the convers<u>at</u>ion
    Clue – <u>sat</u>

12.	GREAT	It's <u>great</u> to <u>eat</u>
	GREATEST	Extend gr<u>eat</u> to gr<u>eat</u>est
13.	DICTATE	a 'lead up' word
		Now use part of dictate for...
	DICTION	careful of /sh/. Extend Diction
	DICTION<u>ARY</u>	it was left in the c<u>ar</u>
14.	INTEREST	speak clearly (syllables) = 'talk to pencil'
	INTERESTING	Extend to interesting
15.	EDUCATE	use most of *educate* for EDUCATION
16.	ATTRACT	careful – one *t* attracts the other *t*
	ATTRACTION	extend *attract* to *attraction*
17.	BEAUTY	dress up … <u>listen</u> for clues in BE - Aunty and Uncle – BEAUTY
18.	TOUR	<u>our</u> t<u>our</u>

Comment in Support of the Above Approach

Here we are teaching children LISTENING and REASONING SKILLS rather than focusing on visual memory (Look-Cover-Write-Check), which does not seem to be any more successful than the alphabet (reciting the letters) approach.

1. Association of ideas – children to LINK new sounds or words to previous experiences. e.g. Dinosaurs – Aunty & Uncle, ran when they saw a Dinosaur.

    Dinos
    - talk to pencil
    - Refer to catchy clues – Aunty & Uncle

2. Children to identify Support Clues in sentences given by Teachers. e.g. GREAT – IT'S GREAT TO EAT.

3. Teacher to break down word to base word e.g. ELECTRICITY, ELECT – Base, ELECTRIC – Extension, ELECTRICITY – Further extension.

4. Teacher to Reinforce Clues at all times.

5. Teacher to record words and clues to encourage children to further develop LISTENING and REASONING SKILLS.

This approach eliminates negative attitudes in children because of the challenging aspect. Spelling becomes fun and successful.

Some sounds are very frequent in their occurrence and confusing in their variety of spellings. In such cases, a whole group of spellings should be treated at once, and the page (or part of it) may be treated as a 'detective' page (see below).

Detective Pages in the Sound Dictionary

The more a child actively and purposefully puzzle over a word, the more likely he is to remember it when he has to work out its spelling. It follows therefore that it is desirable to give clues to as many difficult words as possible, requiring the child to act as a detective and follow up the clues to a correct solution.

Where time is limited, one word-family may be treated at a time. Where more time is available, whole pages of the Sound Dictionary (i.e. all or most of the spellings of one sound) should be treated at one session. Children love the blend of activity, silly clues, puzzles and, most of all, writing a large number of words correctly. Rarely will there be time to do all pages as detective pages, but a list of desirable pages is suggested. (See 'Suggestions for Work', p. 92.)

Silent Letters

Once the regular phonic variations have been understood, the remaining and major problem of English spelling are letters that are silent. Most of us have little problem with such letters, and indeed, we are unaware of how many silent letters there are in English. We can immediately think of the silent e, the most regularly occurring of the silent letters; a little more thought produces the silent b in lamb, limb, etc.; silent p in psalm and psychology; silent k in knife and knuckle; and possibly the silent n in autumn. Psalm reminds us of silent l, (or is it part of the /a/ sound?). Because these are obvious, we have little trouble with them, remembering them as peculiarities. Our remedial children need to have their attention drawn to the peculiarities, and various mnemonic devices may be used to do so.

The less obvious, but more troublesome, silent letter is the one that a literate person thinks they pronounce, but usually doesn't. The following are cases in point: emblem, blossom, animal, camel. To the normal reader, these four words are pronounced just as they are spelt: we would say to the child, "Talk to your pencil." But of course, the child hears, not /emblem/ but emblm, or, just possibly, /emblem/. Blossom has, phonically, one silent s as well as an o that is silent or reduced to an indefinite sound. Most children do not hear the indefinite as a sound, anyway. Animal has a silent a, and the e is silent in camel. However, some dialects, idioms or local pronunciation may vocalise letters, such as the **g** in song by some people of English counties. To help the remedial child cope with such difficulties, it will be necessary to work from auditory and visual and kinaesthetic aspects simultaneously, as far as possible. Before proceeding to consider particular problems, here are some general lines of attack:

Auditory

An exaggerated pronunciation will often help. As we have noted before, the child needs to hear our voice saying the word the way it is to be spelt. Many of us have remembered odd words by facetiously pronouncing the silent letter when we said the word. For our remedial children, during the activity and on the recording, we will pronounce emblem as it is spelt, and thus draw attention to its structure. Only then can we call it a 'talk to pencil' word.

Visual

Such an auditory emphasis will sufficiently assist most children with the simpler silent letters. It is neither possible nor desirable to treat all problems in that way. Sometimes a crudely visual approach will help, for xylophone, to imagine (and draw) the crossed strikers of the xylophone as forming the first letter. More often, we may link the problem to a visual clue and ask the child to work it out for himself. This 'detective' process helps form a lasting impression of the structure of the word in the child's mind.

Kinaesthetic

Mainly through the writing of words. This should be closely related to any visual emphasis, especially for children who have perceptual problems of any kind.

Detective Steps

* Talk to pencil.
* If there is a catch – warn yourself.
* Where do you think the catch is – which sound?
* Sample word – 'special' – look up in index for the catch sound e.g. 'sh' pages 136, 137, Sheet 9 for pictures to 'sh' sound.
* Children copy list into the margin.
* Write 'music' on scrap paper.
* Ask which of the bossy letters works hardest.
* Make 'c' say 'sh'.
* Clue – 'music' – finish musician, underline and colour the two letters that say 'sh'.
* Use the same colour per sound e.g. sh, ti, ce, all pink, etc.
* Now select picture from Sheet 9 and put 'musician' in the correct section.
* Now write 'special' in that section – colour and underline the 'sh' sound.
* Now write 'social' in this section – colour and underline the 'sh' sound.
* To be a detective you need to follow these steps:

1. Think about the word – simple or catchy word.
2. Identify sound.
3. Refer to index for sound and picture.
4. Classify list of sounds in margin on appropriate page.
5. Recall clue word.
6. Organise correct sound to picture.
7. Write whole word in appropriate section.
8. Put in picture.

Suggestions for Work

Teachers may find it useful to note the following suggestions of pages that need to be worked by children of different ages:

For pupils in Grade 3 and below:
a. Sound Group 13 /aʊ/
b. Sound Group 14 /ɔɪ/
c. Sound Group 4 /e/ especially ee, ea.
d. Sound Group 2 /ɛɪ/ especially ay, ai, ey
e. Sound Group 47 /d/

For pupils in Grades 4-6:
a. Sound Groups 25 /L/
b. Sound Groups 20 Treat this page first if early progression to reading is important /ɔ/
c. Letter Based Groups 49 ough Treat this page second if early progression to reading is important.
d. Sound Group 36 /m/
e. Sound Group 37 /n/
f. Sound Groups 39 /ʃ/ Do the whole page with 5th and 6th graders.

Further pages or parts of pages should be treated as they are suggested by words occurring in the week's spelling list.

The following are particularly useful:

Sound Group 18 (air)
Sound Group 19 (eer)
Sound Group 21 (k)
Sound Group 32 (z)
Sound Group 39 (d)
and for older children.
Sound Group 31 (t)
Sound Group 35 (w)

Teaching Points:

Sometimes, marking the word itself will help.

For example, when a pair of vowels occurs, mark the silent one by putting a stroke through it, and indicate the quality of the sounded one by a 'long' or 'short' mark: ā, ē, ă.

In some cases, such marks may be placed on spellings in the margins of the Sound Dictionary.

Jenny's Sound Dictionary

The following points should be noted about the word lists:

1. The size of each list of words gives an indication of the frequency of the spelling in English, though, unfortunately, some infrequently occurring patterns are used in common words (e.g. the eo in people, ew in sew).
2. The words have been chosen with preference for less common words so that pupils may have practice in previously unknown words, with an ensuing increase in confidence. Pupils should be encouraged to 'talk to their pencils', an exercise they will enjoy, having been given one or two necessary clues for catches in harder words.
3. Generally, space has limited lists to twenty words, arranged in columns so as to offer one–, two–, three– and four–syllable words, or so as to use the sound in different parts of the word, so that practice is given in using the spelling in as many different contexts as possible.
4. The result is that many unusual and 'grown-up' words are included. If easier words are required, teachers will find they are often suggested by words given, or that they are already parts of compound words given. Thus, on p. 98 under train, ascertain occurs, and would suggest entertain, though that word is not given. Under play, lay, pay, and, away are not given, but are suggested by overlay, overpay, and, stowaway. Teachers will need to add to the lists.
5. Teachers will find the lists helpful in encouraging students to enlarge their vocabularies, but the big advantage, especially when facilitating reading, will be in having easy reference to words with spelling and phonetic similarity to words the pupil finds difficult.
6. Choice of Categories. Linguistically, one of the most common sounds in English is the indefinite schwa sound /ə/. For this sound, Gattegno lists sixteen different spellings. There is no compelling reason why teachers should not establish an /ə/ page, should they so desire, listing in the margins the spellings: a, u, e, o, io, i, y, ou, oo, eli, ai, eou, ough, ie, iou.

We have taken the view that to observe the structure of the word as well as its sound, it is better for practical purposes to slightly exaggerate the pronunciation and classify these spellings under the nearest useful and definite sound. Thus, insurance is in sound group 2 (a) on page 99, under dance as a clue word. Collar, sailor, and, sister, all appear on the /er/ page as varieties of that sound, though clearly collar could go on the /or/ page, and sailor on the or page.

Classification of words will also vary slightly with a person's accent. Thus, a Scot would put quarrel on the /or/ page, but an Australian would put it on the /o / (orange) page. Such considerations are unimportant so long as the child can pronounce the word clearly, and recognise it when it is pronounced to you.

Phonetic Symbols Used

Throughout this book, reference to the alphabet name of a letter is indicated by the use of italics or underlining: *a*, *b*, etc. or. a, b, etc.

When the sound of a letter is meant, phonetic symbols are used and placed between slashes: / ae /,/ b / etc, or highlighted, ae, b, etc.

The following table gives the approximate value assigned to each symbol. Precise analysis of the sound is not, of course, required.

Symbol	Sound	Symbol	Sound
a	car	m	mice
æ	had	n	nut
aɪ	sigh	ŋ	sing
aʊ	cow	oʊ	so
b	button	ɒ	hot
d	din	ɔ	or
dʒ	jelly	ɔɪ	boy
ɛ	head	p	pin
ɛə	air	r	ran
ɜ	bird	s	snake
eɪ	say	ʃ	show
f	fin	t	tin
g	gate	tʃ	chip
h	head	θ,ð	thin, then
i	seat	u	boot
ɪ	sit	ʊ	book
ɪə	hear	v	vine
j	xes you	ʌ	byt win
ju	at, ettle	w	zoo
k	let	z	measure (zh)
l		ʒ	

Jenny's Sound Dictionary

The Sounds of English and their Spellings

In this table the sounds have been arranged according to their usefulness in teaching remedial reading and spelling. Thus the list is not exhaustive, but still embraces more than will be required by the secondary school pupil. Note that there is no place for the indefinite sound, its various spellings being classified under the nearest sound represented in careful speech.

Figure: 12

Jenny's Sound Dictionary

a (apple)   Sound Group 1

apple

hat

dance	entrance	importance	extravagance	a
trance	distance	appearance	significance	
prance	balance	attendance	acquaintance	
glance	finance	ambulance	circumstance	
	hindrance	reliance	performance	
ant				
chant	migrant	ignorant	insignificant	
pant	remnant	tolerant	superabundant	
grant	constant	observant	communicant	
plant	pageant	defiant	luxuriant	
slant	vacant	reluctant	participant	

plait   ai

plaid

Note: The sound /ae/ presents little difficulty. Words ending in –ant and –ance are a problem, so collecting them here using ant and dance for clues is helpful. See also Sound Group 37 on page 141 of this Sound Dictionary (an). In normal speech, of course, the sound of the a in many of these words is indefinite (schwa) /a/.

a (angel)   Sound Group 2

angel					a
apron dais	apricot donator curator	escalator incubator incinerator			
sundae					ae
gate plate grape chase pane frame create	inhale advantage mistake membrane dictate rename	advantage propagate centigrade stimulate hurricane	congratulate supermundane appropriate substantiate disadvantage		a-e
play bay clay sway spray	display repay array astray dismay		yesterday Saturday overlay overlay stowaway		ay
train paid stain aim fail bait	remain restrain afraid mermaid disdain	preordain porcelain chamberlain ascertain entertain			ai
trait					ait
straight					aigh
gaol					ao
gauge (if needed, put on pg. 147 with other rare irregular words.)					au

a (angel) Sound Group 2

grey				
prey they whey	they	obey convey survey	abeyance Reynard	ey
reins vein veil		skein feint	surveillance reindeer heinous	ei
reign	feign	design		eig
eight freight weigh weight (y) sleigh neigh	eighty eighteen neighbour	outweigh	Our **eigh**t n**eigh**bours My w**eigh**t, **eigh**t kg's, My h**eigh**t, **eigh**t feet.	eigh
break steak great				ea
ballet valet beret chet	bouquet parquet crochet croquet	ricochet tourniquet		et
fete				e

e (egg)   Sound Group 3

hen					e
fed	velvet	excellent	embezzlement		
well	legend	effervesce	benevolent		
hem	tempest	cemented	embellishment		
step	helmet	tenement	enlightenment		
beg	elect	semester			
bread	wealthy	endeavour	leatheriness		ea
meant	feather	pleasantry	pleasantry		
breadth	treasure	treachery			
spread	heaven	measurement			
tread	threading	threatening			

You <u>eat</u> your <u>bread</u> and <u>spread</u> on your <u>bread</u>

A Reading Exercise:
I spread myself out with my head on the heather.
This was to give me a measure of pleasure.
The sky was like lead, and threatened bad weather.
I dreamt about death and heaven and treasure.
I knew that endeavour with thread and good leather would give me
great wealth and surely some treasure.
That bread, baked with leaven as light as a feather would give me
good health and certainly pleasure.
A peasant was I and as deaf as could be, but I read heavy books, for my eyes could
see. I had no dread of ill for my breath was steady, I leapt towards great wealth with
no stealth in my tread.
I hoped for good health, and meant to find wealth, but instead I found
wealth right there in good health.

<u>heifer</u>	their	leisure	leisurely	leisureliness	ei
<u>friend</u>					ie
<u>said</u>					ai
<u>says</u>					ay
<u>many</u>	any	anyone	anything		a
<u>bury</u>					u
<u>leopard</u>					eo
<u>aeroplane</u>					ae
aerobatics					
aerodynamics					
haemorrhage					

Jenny's Sound Dictionary

e (emu)   Sound Group 4

me	sesame	museum			e
he	simile	hideous			
we	acme	courteous			
de...	anemone	plenteous			
pre...	create	stereo (type)			
re...					
trapeze					e-e
cede	concrete	kerosene	supersede		
swede	precede	intervene	extremely		
theme	supreme	indiscrete	discretely		
scheme	stampede	incomplete	serenely		
scene	convene	centipede	intercede		
tree					ee
free	proceed	greenhorn	addressee		
speed	degrees	cheetah	mortgagee		
deep	beseech	leeward	guarantee		
speech	upkeep	seepage	employee		
fleet	decreed	teeming	jamboree		

A ref**ee** wanted to m**ee**t his committ**ee** under a tr**ee** or in a tep**ee** or a marqu**ee**.

He guarant**ee**d that they could have coff**ee** and toff**ee** at the jubil**ee** if they would agr**ee**.

eat					ea
breathe	eager	impeach	cochineal		
beach	easel	displease	interweave		
eagle	teasing	repeat	misdemeano (u) r		
feast	neatly	bereave	predecease		
please	feature	conceal	underneath		

My Dream Called 'e-a'. In the h**ea**t of summer in my dr**ea**m I l**ea**d a t**ea**m of b**ea**vers towards a gl**ea**m. They go **ea**st with the str**ea**m till they r**ea**ch the s**ea**, so far ben**ea**th a p**ea**ceful b**ea**ch. They **ea**t m**ea**t and b**ea**ns on a s**ea**t called a b**ea**m. While one of them sp**ea**ks they have p**ea**ches and cr**ea**m. This tr**ea**t of a m**ea**l, to say the l**ea**st, would fatten the l**ea**n for it's r**ea**lly a f**ea**st. When filled to the s**ea**ms they're ever so pl**ea**sed. Then in my dr**ea**m, when going to l**ea**ve, I make b**ea**vers repeat that **ea** says /ee/ . That's what I t**ea**ch when they're standing at **ea**se: that **ea** says /ee/, and they think I'm a t**ea**se!

Sound Group 4

people				eo
quay				oe
phoenix				ay
debris	chassis	verdigris	louis (d' or)	is
encyclopaedia	algae	antennae	formulae	haemoglobin	ae
taxi fiord kiosk kiwi suite	medium sardine routine machine serious	champion obedient tangerine serviette previous	convenient experience enthusiastic appropriate immediately	i
piano baby story handy plenty tidy	memory angry shivery argosy revelry	recovery discovery immunity chivalry eternity	solidarity peculiarity popularity familiarity copyright	y
key monkey medley barley chutney	lackey motley blarney hackney cockney	hokey-pokey blarney		ey

A Sydney jockey on a donkey went on a journey through a valley. He had money in a trolley for hockey in an alley, and a ball game of volley! He saw a chimney on an abbey, a pulley in a two-storey galley, a turkey with some parsley in a kidney, and a monkey in a jersey eating honey with a key.

Sound Group 4

ceiling	conceive	conceivable	casein	ei
deceive	protein	perceivable	caffeine	
receive	mortein			
receipt				

> You **seize** your prize as well as the e before i.
> You **seize** prot**ein** for your health,
> You **seize** Mort**ein** for the flies.

chief

> Mostly i before e, except after c.

ie

brief	achieve	achievement
shriek		
frieze		hygiene

<u>A Siege</u> A ch**ie**f caught a young th**ie**f in a f**ie**ld. Gr**ie**f changed to rel**ie**f when a misch**ie**vous th**ie**f had to y**ie**ld up his sh**ie**ld to a ch**ie**f in a f**ie**ld. He was glad to bel**ie**ve in the pr**ie**st's repr**ie**ve.

i (igloo)   Sound Group 5

igloo hint pink grip slid twin	habit digit picnic fillip tipping	optimist minimum criticism prohibit	intimidate diminishing incivility implicitly	invisibility	i
pyjamas myth gypsy cygnet system symbol	syrup crystal symptom syringe cymbal	platypus disyllable methylated synomym (ous)	amethyst antonym anonymous metonymy analyst		y
pretty	comedy * benefit * vinegar tragedy*	privilege antelope * competent * barbecue	society appetite * enemy *		e
sieve					ie
forfeit					ei
busy	lettuce	minute			u
build		biscuit circuit			ui

u and i can't b**ui**ld, we must engage a b**ui**lder

vehicles	exhibit	exhibitor exhibition			hi
vehement					he
women					o

i (ice) — Sound Group 6

ice violin trial bisect spiral gastritis	spiral compliance inscribing collided appendicitis	arthritis tonsillitis hepatitis meningitis				i
pie tie	lie	die	magpie			ie
line	ride wife spike price snipe	oblige polite confide reside	missile	expedite advertise compromise enterprise intertwine		i-e
fly shy pry style type	cyclone pylon xylophone dynamics hypothesis	enzyme analyse paralyse prototype electrolyte	intensify disqualify amplify simplify pacify			y
buy		guy	buying			uy
light righteous	thigh foresight	blight sprightly	upright			igh

I go **high** to fix the **light**.

height	sleight (of hand)					eigh
eye						eye
dye	stye	goodbye				ye
island	isle					is
aisle						ais
eiderdown	either *	einstein	kaleidoscope			ei

Some people say '**e**-ther' and some say **i**-ther, so put both **e** and **i**.

Jenny's Sound Dictionary

o (orange) — Sound Group 7

					o
<u>dog</u>					
loss	doctor	lemonade	lollipop	rhinoceroses	
bond	sponsor	horology	golliwog	trigonometry	
flop	tosses	colonise	apricot	anthropology	
prod	poppy	mnemonic	paragon	chronology	
jog	rocking	harmony	anthropoid	animosity	

				a
<u>watch</u>				
was	swallow	squadron	quality	
wasp	washable	squalid	quantity	
want	squashing	quarrel*	disqualify	
squat	wander	wallow**	wallaby	

*The / ō / is really ar here. **The / ō / is really al.

			au
<u>Australia</u>			
sausage	auction	cauliflower	
austere	caustic	hydraulic	
laurel	assault		

	ou
<u>cough</u>	
trough (see also Letter-Based Groups, p. 146)	

		oh
<u>John</u>	demi-john	

		ho
<u>honest</u>		
honest	honestly	
honourable	honorary	
honesty	honorarium	

	eo
<u>luncheon</u>	
truncheon	

	ow
<u>knowledge</u>	
rowlock	

		oa
<u>broad</u>	broadcast	abroad

o (open) — Sound Group 8

open roll hold post comb	progress coheir go-cart vocal	monogram desolate pantomime melody	portfolio embargo volcano flamingo	albino	o

It felt like zero by the silo.
A merino listened to the solo.
Was there a banjo and piano, or only an alto and soprano?

Just add s for the plural. When is it es?

toe hoe woe	foe floe	oboe throe	mistletoe tiptoe	goes	oe
hose code rose drove globe rope	compose microbe promote misquote corrode	microphone telescope episode rigmarole antidote	kaleidoscope anticyclone		o-e
boat load foam groan soak soap		refloat encroach scapegoat waistcoat bemoan	petticoat overcoat stagecoach cockroach approach	roadworthy unloading soapy gloating toasted	oa
snow crow mow flow glow tow	rainbow elbow swallow minnow barrow	fellowship narrowing sorrowing widower following	foreshadow overthrow bungalow undertow overgrown		ow
owe					ot
depot sabot		entrepot	haricot (beans etc.)		ot
brooch					oo

o (open)   Sound Group 8

plateau tableau trousseau	tonneau	beau tonneau	chateau	eau
oh!				oh
sew				ew
boatswain				oat
yeoman				eo
shoulder		remould		ou
dough	furlough	though	brougham	ough
mould	smoulder	boulder		

Should I shoulder the boulder?

(see also Letter-Based Groups pg. 146)

u (umbrella) — Sound Group 9

umbrella				apparatus	u
up	puffin	album	pendulum	hippopotamus	
bus	subway	stirrup	hibiscus	auditorium	
fuss	hubbub	walnut	prospectus	eucalyptus	
junk	fungus	nimbus	thesaurus	metatarsus	
mother					o
some	money	among	wonderful		
month	comely	another	company		
front	colour		comfortable		
monk	oven		covering		
tongue	Monday				
(o -o -hugs for mother)					
country (our)					ou
couple	cousin	famous	generous	ambiguous	
double	nourish	callous	coniferous	mountainous	
trouble	flourish	spacious	frivolous	ridiculous	
does		(See Building Spelling Cleverness, p. 72)			oe
flood					oo
blood		flood			
'Good blood'					
cupboard					up
around					a
alive	father		sofa	vanilla	
about	dance		extra	media	
above	above		copra		
abrupt	abrupt		dogma	propaganda	
among	among		comma		

Note:
The sound / ʌ / presents many problems. Words ending in -us (nouns) or -ous (adjectives) may be 'put away' on this page.
The sound / ʌ / at the beginning of many words and at the end of most words is spelt a. These words should be put away here, too.

u (uniform) — Sound Group 10

music uniform unit union usurp unite	unicorn unify united universe unison	monument pendulum insulate luxury ambulance	matriculate perpetual meticulous particular perpendicular	u
statue due cue sue hue pursue	value issue rescue argue residue	continue revenue barbecue avenue	discontinue undervalue	ue
tune cube mute tube fuse mule	confuse transfuse refuge rebuke globule	substitute introduce contribute longitude ridicule	ingratitude redistribute hypotenuse centrifuge superinduce	u-e
queue (long line of boys and girl: ue ue ue ue)				ueue
nuisance suitor suitable suitcase 'U and I are a nuisance at the dance'	pursuit recruit conduit			ui
adieu	lieu	purlieu		ieu
view preview	review	interview		iew

news hewn stew newt drew few	mildew sinew curfew nephew renew	skewer pewter steward ewer newel	sewerage		ew
ewe			awe		ewe
Europe neuter Euclid feudal euchre feud	neutralise eucalypt eulogy neurosis eurhythmics	pneumonia neurology neutrality pneumati	Europe		eu
you	youth				you
beauty	beautiful	'Be A beaUt, Mum'			eau

oo (book) Sound Group 11

book stood crook foot shook nook	forsook overlook falsehood childhood barefoot	goodness footstool tenderfoot neighbourhood misunderstood		oo
could would	should	(See Infants Words in Building Spelling Cleverness, p. 72)		oul
pull pussy push (er) bush full bull	pudding pulley pulpit pullet bullet	bushel butcher fulfil (see also Sound Group 25, pg.131) skilfully		u
wolf Wollongong woman				o

Jenny's Sound Dictionary

oo (hoop) — Sound Group 12

hoop				oo
woo	monsoon	nincompoop	hullabaloo	
scoop	teaspoon	pantaloon	peek-a-boo	
groove	mushroom	macaroon	cockatoo	
snooze	festoon	waterproof	shampoo	
mood	whirlpool	bandicoot	bamboo	

Lose and Loose: My buttons are loose.
(Two buttons, long threads of o s. Lose a button? Lose an o.)

rheumatism	eu

to			o
do	loser	undo	
lose	proving	remove	
who	mover		
move*			

* Move: How many refrigerators could you? Only one.

shoe		oe
	canoe	

*Shoe: Can't put two o s, because you lost one (shoe) and bossy Mum (e) was cross!

two	wo

soup				ou
group	routine	recoup	cantaloup	
route	tourist	caribou		
wound	louis (d'or)		troubadour	
rouge				

ruler					u
June	ruin	jubilee	instrument	jubilantly	
flute	fluent	supervise	protruding	duplication	
jube	rumour	juvenile	included	fluorescent	
funeral	cruet	scrutiny	seclusion	jurisdiction	
cruel	plural	fluency	enthusiastic		

manoeuvre	oeu

blue cue clue true flue	sue Glue the clue, (blue), to true.	accrue construe	misconstrue	ue
jewel grew screw drew threw	screwing beshrew	jewellery		ew
through	through (see also Letter-Based Groups, p.146)			ough
fruit sit juice must cruise	bruised suitable recruit	You (u) and I like fruit. You and I wear suits. You and I, my dear penguin, not ruin our suits with bruised fruit or juice on the cruise.		ui
pleurisy	rheumatic	rheumatism		eu

ow (owl) — Sound Group 13

owl howl frown growl clown crowd	drowsy prowler coward trowel rowdy	renown allowed eyebrow sundown endow	glowering allowing empower dowry overpower	ow
house (our) our oust cloud bounce sprout	sprouted sounding loutish doubtful mountain	resounding profoundly confounded announcement abounding	greyhound compound aground astound renounce	ou

A proud mouse went out round about our house. He found a mound of pounds upon the ground. With his mouth he counted them and never made a sound. Then a cloud in the south and the sight of a grouse made him shout out aloud and go off with a bound.

hour hourly		hou
You need a chair(h) if you've to wait for an hour.		
plough (see also Letter-Based Groups, p. 146)		ough
drought bough		
'our' words for faster recall*		

our   age has   courage
        on   our   honour
        in   our   favour
             our   favourite   flavour
      for   our   nourishment
             our   eight   neighbours
    see   our   behaviour
   hear   our   clamour
   notice our adour and   fervour
   Mother likes our   colours
   our   keys for the court
               out   courtesy
               our   journey
                           demeanour
*based, of course, on spelling, not sound. endeavour		

oy (boy)   Sound Group 14

boy					oy
toy	boycott	employment	corduroy		
troy	oyster	enjoying	saveloy		
coy	royal	disloyal	viceroy		
joy	voyage	flamboyant	gargoyle		
annoy	soy	annoyance			
coin					oi
hoist	ointment	avoiding	hydrofoil		
poise	moisture	embroider	counterfoil		
choice	coinage	exploiter	disembroil		
quoit	jointly	appointment	maladroit		
join	pointer	anointed			
buoy					uoy

r (rabbit)   Sound Group 15

				r
<u>rabbit</u>				
drag	shrapnel	pilgrimage		
crest	stresses	outrageous		
grill	sprinkling	congregate		
trot	shrove-tide	represent		
brush	scrubbing	description		
<u>parrot</u>				rrx
parrot	error	terrier		
berry	errand	porringer		
scurry	torrid	sorrowing		
barrel	terror	merrier		
marrow	porridge	quarrelling		
mirror				
<u>write</u>				wr
wrap	wrongfully	wretchedness		
wrench	wringing	overwrought		
wrist	wrinkly			
wrath	wrangler			
wreck	writhing			
<u>rhombus</u>				rh
rhyme	rhubarb	rhetoric		
rhythm	rhomboid	rheostat		
		rheumatism		
		rhinoceros		
		rhododendron		

ar (car)   Sound Group 16

					ar
car					
star	target	embargo	exhilarate		
arm	partner	departed	oligarchic		
dart	charter	retarded	oviparous		
sharp	barber	escarpment	patriarch		
yard	harpoon	enlargement	standard		
galah					ah
bah	rajah	verandah	hallelujah		
ah	punkah	Messiah			
	loofah				
	hurrah				
aunt					au
	Aunt and Uncle (au).				
father					a
task	casket	giraffe		epitaph	
bask	fasten	mirage			
bath	pastor	moustache			
half	pasture	charade		raspberry	
grasp	psalm	barrage			
My Father: His **task** is to take a **bask**et to the **cast**le and to **ask** for a plant in a **bath** or a **vase**. My father would rather **fasten** his calm **calf** to the **palm** but he can't because of the **brass** band. He takes his calm **calf fast past** a flag at half **mast**. At **last** for my father a drink of **raspberry** in a **glass** and he sits on the **grass** by the **class**.					
are	Bossy Mum says, "Where *are* you?"				are
heart					ear
hearth	hearty				
	hearken				
clerk		sergeant			er
nougat					at
bazaar					aar
bizarre	The bazaar was bizarre.				arre
catarrh					arrh

Jenny's Sound Dictionary

er Sound Group 17

flower					er
her	clever	person	observer	unilateral	
per	number	sermon	emperor	probationer	
	cloister	fertile	funeral	upholsterer	
timber		perplex	federal	collateral	
bumper	her flower	perfect	sorcerer	supervisor	
		persuade		recuperate	
transferred					err
preferred					
referred					
learn					ear
search	earnest	rehearsal			
yearn	earldom	earthliness			
pearl	earthward	earnestly			
hearse	earthen	searchingly			
heard	earthquake				

I **hear**d if you y**ear**n for l**ear**ning and rise **ear**ly to s**ear**ch **ear**nestly and reh**ear**se at each reh**ear**sal, you **ear**n p**ear**ls on **ear**th.

were	'we were'			ere
fire				re
spire	acre	umpire	kilometre	
lyre	fibre	perspire	manoeuvre	
tyre	sombre	retire	calibre	
hire	meagre	transpire	mediocre	
theatre	conspire	massacre		

The Ogre Fire:
There was a fi**re** by a theat**re**.
Ty**re**s we**re** on fi**re** in the cent**re** of an ac**re** of land.
Fi**re**men we**re** desi**re**d and hi**re**d: they we**re** inspi**re**d, admi**re**d.
Police we**re** requi**re**d at the fi**re** to enqui**re**. They we**re** all ti**re**d, of the og**re** fi**re**.

bird				ir
sir	astir	skirmish	elixir	
fir	bestir	chirping	respiration	
skirt		smirking	aspirin	
twirl			affirmative	
mirth			aspiration	

Birds and Circles
Look! A nest, f**ir**m in a f**ir** tree. Mother b**ir**d c**ir**cles, baby b**ir**ds ch**ir**p, Mother b**ir**d st**ir**s and st**ir**s, baby b**ir**ds wh**ir**l, sw**ir**l and tw**ir**l. F**ir**st b**ir**d sits on a sh**ir**t. Next one stands on a sk**ir**t, Th**ir**d one settles on d**ir**t. What m**ir**th! They all find water that squ**ir**ts. Squ**ir**t the d**ir**ty b**ir**d. All are ast**ir**, the g**ir**l and s**ir**. B**ir**ds and c**ir**cles.

Sound Group 17

				yr
martyr				
	satyr			
	zephyr	martyr		

	yrrh
myrrh	

				ar
collar*				
pillar	farther	circular		
solar	orchard	infirmary		
dollar	drunkard			
standard	the	nearest	definite	

*The sound is usually, of course, indefinite. The words should be put away under sound: either here or with Sound Group 16, on p. 116 (ar).

			or
world			
worm	worship	foreword	
worse	wordy	catchword	
worth	doctor	watchword	
work	motor	mirroring	
worst	pallor	conductor	

			our*
journey			
	scourge	labourer	
	journal	candour	
	courteous	colour	
		valour	
		favour	

See also Sound Group 20 on p. 120 if / ɔ / pronunciation preferred for colour.
* Letter-Based Groups p. 146 for more words using clue 'our'.

	olo
colonel	

Jenny's Sound Dictionary

church				ur
surf	sturdy	disturb	reimburse	
urge	further	murmur	survivors	
purse	survey	outburst	urgently	
curl	Thursday	upsurge	nursery	
lurk	surgeon	unfurl	pursuers	

I take my purse on purpose, to pursue the thing I want to purchase.

purr				urr
burr	demurred	occurred		
	slurred			
	furry			

figure		ure
conjure	disfigure	
fissure	leisure	

air — Sound Group 18

chair	and I run to...			air
stair	dairy	impair	disrepair	
flair	hairy	eclair	debonair	
fair	fairy	mohair	repairing	
pair	despair	unfair	despairing	
lair	repair	affair		

A **pair** of **fair haired dairy** boys sat on a **chair**. They fell down the **stairs** and were in desp**air** for they couldn't rep**air** the **chair**. What an aff**air**! Until a **fairy** came out of her **lair** and did the rep**air**. (She had a fl**air** for rep**air**!)

scarecrow				are
flare	warfare		compare	earthenware
spare	ensnare		declare	thoroughfare
			prepare	unaware
square	outdare			threadbare
fare	nightmare			ploughshare
beware				

Car, take **care**! Star, don't st**are**! Go far, pay a f**are**. On the bar, feet b**are**. Only a scar, no sc**are**! Do not spar, please sp**are**. Do not mar your m**are**. I'm aw**are** a r**are** h**are** d**are**s gl**are** at sc**are**crows. I decl**are** he said in the squ**are** just to sh**are** and comp**are** the w**are**s prepared. Take c**are**!
Take a boss (e), to drive a car with c**are**.

Jenny's Sound Dictionary

				aire
millionaire	questionnaire	commissionaire		
Mary vary wary		scaring glaring sparing daring	preparing comparing declaring	vegetarian octogenarian	ar
Contrary Mary is wary, and does not vary. She's caring and sparing and daring.				
bear tear pear wear	outwear outswear bugbear	overbearing forebear forbearanc		ear
A bear eats a pear and tears the clothes he wears.				
where	there			ere
their			heir	eir
prayer	heir (take off the t)			ayer
mayor				ayor
aeroplane	aerial	aerodrome	aerobatics	aer

eer Sound Group 19

					eer
deer	cheer steering peerage	sneer veneer career	profiteer auctioneer		
steer jeer	deerhound seersucker	overseer volunteer	domineer mountaineer		
The Deer and the Engineer: An engineer will volunteer to pioneer and be a mountaineer. He'll cheer the deer and steer the deer if they have beer and begin to career as if they are agree. He will not sheer nor be a mutineer. This engineer will be a seer, a pioneer.				
ear clear spear rear smear year	earmark earwig tearful fearsome gearbox	appear arrears endear besmear headgear	disappearance overhearing endearment endearingly		ear

here					ere
Doctor, I'm sinc**ere**. The pain is sev**ere** h**ere** and it's m**ere**ly a sph**ere** but I'll persev**ere** if you don't interf**ere** with the atmosph**ere**!					
cereal	serial	inferior		stereotype	er
era	serum	exterior			
hero	period	superior			
zero	serious				
Nero					
pier		cashier	chandelier		ier
ierce		gondolier			
frontier		chiffonier			
pierce		fiercest	cavalier	fusilier	
bier					
weir	weird	weirdly			eir
souvenir					ir

or   Sound Group 20

horse				or
horn	forward	remorse	assortment	
cord	mortal	forlorn	subordinate	
form	fortune	abhor	extortion	
born	torment	corridor	disorderly	
lord	dormant	metaphor	scorpion	
sore	foreshore	encore	stevedore	ore
more	foresight	fourscore	pinafore	
chore	forecast	explore	commodore	
score	forego	ignore	semaphore	
lore	scorer	therefore	sycamore	
fore				

More About Sore and Bob: This boy Bob did his mother ad**ore**, yet mother's advice did Bob ign**ore**, for he wanted to go to the sh**ore** to expl**ore**. The shoes Bob w**ore**, alas, they t**ore**! He went to the st**ore** with feet so s**ore**, for plasters gal**ore** he did impl**ore**, but m**ore** and m**ore** Bob did depl**ore** bef**ore** his feet he could rest**ore**!

oar					oar
soar		boarder	surfboard	uproarious	
hoarse		hoarded	uproar	coarseness	
hoard		hoarseness	cardboard	oarsmanship	
coarse		roaring	cupboard		
boar		coarsely	starboard		
mortgage					ort
pour					our
four	fourteen	splendour*	(mis)behaviour		
mourn	mournful	humour	(dis)honour		
course	coursing	glamour	endeavour		
court	courtly	saviour	(mis)demeanour		

*See also Sound Group 17, p. 117 our if / er / pronunciation is preferred for the words in the last two columns.

door					oor
floor	doorstep	indoor	floorwalker		
poorly	outdoor	boorishness	moor		
poor	mooring				
boor	flooring				

sure			
surely	insure	insurance	

You've had a fire, so you (U) rush everywhere to be sure to insure the property and assure the future.

thought	(see also **Letter**-Based Groups, p. 146)				ough
ought	bought	thoughtful	thoughtfulness		
	brought				

I thought they said, "oh, you go home!" (o-u-g-h)

or (ii) — Sound Group 21

paw				aw
claw	awful	rickshaw		
thaw	awkward	outlaw		
lawn	awning	pawpaw		
sprawl	lawyer	withdraw		
squawk	trawler	seesaw		
awe	awesome			awe
auntie & uncle (autumn)				au
automatic				
auditorium				

You had to sweep up the autumn leaves because auntie and uncle were coming for tea. They like sauce with their meal.

Jenny's Sound Dictionary

<u>fault</u> jaunt taunt flaunt staunch	laundry saunter autumn cautious augment austere	defaulting assaulted applauding tarpaulin thesaurus precaution	plausibility authenticity nautical		au
<u>war</u> swarm dwarf warp wharf quart	reward forewarn award toward awkward	warder warbling thwarted quarterly	enthralled forestalling recalled		ar
<u>wall</u> chalk waltz squall bald	almost also already alter although	walrus scalded walnut instalment			a (1)

My clue is all. What do I do to all to make all say bald or waltz, or halter or scald? I'll end with salt, but you must not halt till you know about all because all can talk.

<u>caught</u> taught haughty	(see also Letter-Based Groups, p. 146) naughty slaughter daughter				augh
<u>dinosaur</u> minotaur					aur
<u>exhaust</u> exhaustion					hau
<u>water</u>					a

k (i)   Sound Group 21

<u>kitten</u> skin task keg sank	skipper skittish kelpie sketchy skewer	casket trinket turkey silky hawking	musketeer handkerchief murkiness kerosene skeleton		k
<u>cake</u> spike choke duke	pancake rebuke provoke turnpike earthquake	artichoke undertake ladylike overtake wide-a-wake			ke

See also the word list for Refrence Book P. 63-66.

walk chalk talk	folk yolk			(l) k
khaki khan	khedive	gymkhana		kh
trekked				kk
queen squib quest quiz quell quote	require liquid frequent request inquire	qualify quality quandary squanderer squeamishness	inquisitive requisite acquisition acquaintance frequency	q
quoits quay quoin	marquee liquor	mosquito liquorice conqueror	mannequin etiquette masquerade	qu
cheque mosque plaque pique brusque	opaque unique oblique antique	grotesque physique technique burlesque	picturesque humoresque	que

k **Sound Group 21**

cat cog cup cart cash camel	escape locate coconut cactus crocus	cascaded percolate conclusive incorrect reconstru	cavalcade lubricate nautical massacre ct medical	ecstatic statistic acoustic Antarctic characteristic	c
account occur hiccup mecca succulent accordion	accurate moccasin occasion	tobacco morocco sirocco stucco impeccable	malacca accommodate accumulate accomplish occasional	cc
duck track crock tick pluck sack	picket reckless rocket tackling knick-knack	padlock Matlock attack cassock limerick	mackintosh acknowledge backwardness mackerel checkmate	ck

124 Jenny's Sound Dictionary

school ache choir chasm echo chord Christmas	chorus chemist scholar vchaotic chronic	chloroform chiropractor chiropodist chrysalis chronicle	orchestra anarchist archaic synchronize architecture	ch

Children go to school. There they sing in the choir.

acquire acquit acquaint	acquiesce acquaintance	acquisitive	cq

racquet lacquer		cqu

saccharine Bacchus	bacchant	bacchanalian	cch

k   Sound Group 22

snakes sash spats stilts socks sets	suspect sister spinster sponsor escape	subsidy distrust resistance subsistence subscription	synthesis stethoscope synopsis metamorphosis thrombosis	s
case tense chase glimpse course	expanse eclipse response carcase	universe intersperse predecease merchandise	hypotenuse apocalypse	se

I'm d**ense** if I forget that imm**ense** exp**ense** creates int**ense** susp**ense** and makes no s**ense** or nons**ense**.

dress miss cross fuss ass puss	assess address emboss hostess distress	dismissal embarrassing retrogressive predecessor repossessing	indistinctness outspokenness defencelessness characterless temporariness	ss
			Possess possesses two double sses.	

					sw
sword	answer	swordfish	swordsman		
	"Swing your sword".				

					st
listen (ten times)					
castle	rustling		epistle	chastening	
trestle	wrestling		fasteners	christening	
gristle	whistling		moistening	glistening	
jostle	bristling		listener		
bustle	mistletoe		hastening		

	sth
asthma	
isthmus	

				ps
psalm				
psychic	psalmist	psoriasis	psychology	
			psychopath	
			pseudonym	

			sse
crevasse			
finesse			
	impasse	palliasse	
	lacrosse		

Sound Group 22

s

				c (e)
cent, fence				
space	accept	certificate	reinforce	
since	receive	cenotaph	precipice	
force	precede	cemetery	introduce	
dunce	recent	censorship	frontispiece	
bounce	decent	centimetre	mispronounce	

				c (i)
city, pencil				
cinder	council	incinerator	germicide	
cider	acid	incidental	exercise	
circus	concise	incipient	suicide	
cinch	precise	civilian	coincide	
circuit	decide	civility	convincing	

				c (y)
cycle, tricycle				
cygnet	cyclamin	bicycle	diplomacy	
cymbal	cyanide	tricycle	pharmacy	
cyclist	cylinder	supremacy	piracy	
fancy	cynosure	encyclical	legacy	
mercy	cynical	encyclopaedia		

				sc
scythe	descend	oscillate	effervescent	
scenery	rescind	condescend	convalescence	
scent	crescent	plebiscite	phosphorescent	
science	transcend	quiescent	reminiscent	

				sce
convalesce reminisce effervesce	acquiesce fluoresce coalesce	phosphoresce incandesce		

Problem Letter Combinations

			cess
princess necessary access process	excess success	intercession predecessor	

	ence
busy 'ence' * learn Sound Group 5 'ense' and call everything else busy 'ence'.	

	ance
occurance occupance	

gun   Sound Group 23

					g
gun gag gang grip glebe engulf	fragrant progress gargoyle magnet pentagon	omega monogram flamingo gelignite gregarious	Gorgonzola gargantuan mahogany obligation		
trigger giggle waggle juggle wriggle	stagger goggles luggage gagging	struggling braggart lagging maggot	bedraggled outrigger doggedly raggedly		gg
guide guy guest* guild guard		guitar guiltless guidance guernsey guinea guessed	beguile disguise safeguard rearguard	guillotine guarantee guerilla guardian	gu

* Special work on **gues**s: **gues**sed, **gues**t and **ques**t.

				gh
ghost ghat ghee	gherkin ghetto ghastly gharry ghazi	aghast dinghy	ghostliness	

					gue
plague					
rogue	intrigue	dialogue	pedagogue		
vague	fatigue	monologue			
morgue	prologue	catalogue			
league	colleague	epilogue			
vogue	synagogue				

Sound Group 24

jug	jacket	banjo	justify	disjointed	j
jest	jerky	conjure	janitor	conjunction	
jam	jingle	major	juvenile	conjuror	
jig	junket	prejudice	jaguar	bubbly-jock	
cage		merger	vegetarian		g (e)
change	gentle	anchorage			
gent	Gentile	sergeant	submerged		
large	ginger	pageantry	subterfuge		
genius	pigeon	engagement	sewerage		
general	gorgeous				
giraffe					g (i)
giant	fragile	regiment	vigilance	strategist	
giblets	raging	agility	tragically	geologist	
gibber	digit	regional	agitation	psychologist	
ginger	rigid	agitate	gigantic	archeologist	
gym					g(y)
gypsum	bulgy	gymnasium	ecology		
gyve	clergy	gymkhana	elegy		
gymnast	spongy	gyroscope	effigy		
gyrate	dingy	strategy	prodigy		
suggest					gg
bridge					dge
budget	porridge	fledgeling	foreknowledge		
lodger	partridge	hedgehog	acknowledge		
gadget	abridged	cudgelling	misjudgement		
ledger	dislodged	drudgery	hodge-podge		
judge	adjudged	bludgeon			
A judge sat behind a hedge on the edge of a ledge by the ridge of the bridge. He ate porridge with knowledge.					dg
(midget, ledger, fidget, badger: see above, dge)					

				dj
adjust				
adjoin	adjective	adjustment		
adjourn	adjacent	adjournment		
adjunct	adjutant	readjustment		

	di
soldier	
"I sold my soldier."	

I (contrary) — Sound Group 25

full				fill
fulfil				

				full
skill				
true	skilful			
truly	skilfully			
whole	slowly			
wholly	gradually			
(role, hole)	beautifully			

					roll
roll		enrol	enrolled	enrolment	
	unroll	control	controlling		
		patrol	patrolled		

				tell
tell	retell	excel	excellent	
		travel	traveller	
		jewel	jewellery	
		rebel	rebellious	

Short words, two ls, longer words lose an l, add some more, add an l.

all at the end of words:	mostly all ls, sometimes one l.		-all
recall	pall	install (-ing)	
	appal	instal (-ment)	

all at the beginning of words:	making one word, one l.		al-
almost	almighty	almanac	
already	altogether	always	although (see Letter-Based
altar	alteration	alternate	Groups p. 146)

all as a separate word:			all
	all right	all wrong	

	il
tranquil	
distil	
instil	

<u>wilful</u> hopeful grateful wasteful harmful watchful	dutiful merciful beautiful	purposeful remorseful distasteful reproachful disdainful wonderful		full
<u>gambol</u> carol extol				ol
<u>tunnel</u> channel shrivel bevel	level shovel marvel swivel repel	unravel counsel dishevel		el

Sound Group 25

<u>lamp</u> flannelette geniality vandalism	venality vigilant civility	symbolize paralleled		l
<u>chlorophyll</u> vacillate parallel				ll
<u>elephant</u> celery elegance elevator celebrate	delegate skeleton elect elegy	elect electric electricity accelerate		(ele)
<u>colony</u> colossal biology theology dolomite	apology geology solo(ist) golosh Solomon	symbologist phraseology pharmacologist meteorology	polo polonaise	(olo)
<u>balance</u> salad salary valance	stalactite avalanche			(ala)
<u>agility</u> ability vilify silica	gentility civility military militant	nobility servility		(ili)

l (ii) Sound Group 25

candle twinkle angle table	gamble gentle dangle	trample sample simple		le
camel angel travel counsel novel swivel morsel	**The Colonel:** A colonel wearing flannel from a barrel shovels gravel. On a camel travels level with an angel in a parcel. He finds jewels and a towel in a funnel by a tunnel, and this colonel wearing flannel never quarrels with his camel.			el
animal annual local central	original nominal nominal			al
pencil stencil civil council	civil April peril	The small pencil represents the **i**, and the large pencil represents the **l**.		il
carol petrol gambol symbol idol				ol
gazelle belle	Moselle			lle

Sound Group 26

fish fluff fifty flip fox	fifth forty favour finger	reproof engulf herself twelfth	unfairly disfavour disfigure profusion	waterproof misbeliefo verleaf handkerchief*	f
knife safe chafe	housewife vouchsafe				fe

					ff
coffee					
fluff	offer	sheriff	officer	effective	
cuff*	offence	tariff	ruffian	effeminate	
staff	riffraff	plaintiff	raffia	affirmative	
cliff	bluff	handcuff	rebuffed	affected	
giraffe					ffe
phone					ph
phlox	orphan	pharmacy	cenotaph		
photo	hyphen	physical	epitaph		
phonics	siphon	philosophy	telegraph		
phantom	dolphin	phenomenon	cardiograph		
phase	typhoon	philanthropist	catastrophe		
rough					gh
tough	laughter	draughtsman	enough		
cough	tougher	toughened	laughing		
laugh	coughed	coughing	roughened		
draught	roughage	roughness			
soften	often	oftener	softener		ft
half					lf
calf	calfskin	halfback	behalf		
halfpenny					
halfwit					
lieutenant					u
sapphire	sapphirine				pph
* Plurals:	The **chief**'s handker**chief**s blew from the roof to the cliffs.				

v   Sound Group 27

					v
van					
valve	clover	violin	eleven		
velvet	haven	violent	enliven		
oven	liver	visible	envisage		
seven	quaver	volatile	survival		
vacant	proven	vilify	dissolve		

Jenny's Sound Dictionary

twelve loaves* shelves dove stove pave delve twelve	captive involve revive motive active absolve resolve involve dissolve	detective objective secretive tentative positive	locomotive primitive competitive inquisitive inattentive		ve
halves* calves salve					(1) ve
of					f
nephew	Stephen				ph

* -ves plurals:

> 'Wol**ves** and thie**ves** steal loa**ves** from whar**ves**.

th (voiceless)   Sound Group 28

three thrill thin thing throng thank	fifth sixth twelfth depth width	path length heath wreath thermometer	thirteenth thirtieth diphthong ophthalmia	**3**	th
		th (voiced)			th
clothes this then than thou those these them	thus thine there theirs therefore though thence	bathe other thither whither tether heather	scythe clothe		

Last Thursday they thought that Thor threw thunder at the thief over there. This time, though, I think he threatened to throw three thousand thorny thistles at those other thirsty, thieving thieves.

sh (1)   Sound Group 29

ship shade shed shop shut shy	finish relish selfish varnish refresh	worshipped dishevelled brandished publisher polisher	diminish admonish extinguish impoverish macintosh	sh
cushion cushion cushioning		fashion	fashionable	shi
It's the fa**sh**ion to have a cu**sh**ion in the car.				
extension mansion pension version tension	expansion extension dimension expulsion	comprehension apprehension condescension		si
pressure assure fissure	assurance	reassuringly		ss
discussion mission fission	possession confession admission omission	expression concession obsession concussion	impression profession permission compression	ssi
unconscious conscious luscious		conscionable conscience		sci
conscientious				sc
sugar sure	surely surety	insure insurance		s

sh(ii)

					ti
composition					
mention	invention	examination		fabrication	
action	prevention	explanation		humiliation	
auction	venetian	indication		specification	
patient	Alsatian	publication		personification	
motion	fictitious	dedication		confidential	
Don't men**tion** the composi**tion**!					

					ci
musician					
special	commercial			inefficient	
social	tenacious			insufficient	
spacious	audacious			coefficient	
gracious	precocious			beneficiary	
precious	optician			electrician	

				ce
ocean				
testacean	herbaceous	crustacean	cetacean	

					ch
machine					
chef	chalet	machine	chandelier		
chute	charade	crochet	char-a-banc		
chaise	chamois	ricochet	chivalry		
chagrin	chateau	parachute			
	champagne				

	che
moustache	

		xi
anxious		
noxious	inflexion	
	luxury	
	(see Letter-Based Groups p.146)	

ch — Sound Group 30

chop chin chart choke check impeachment	chapter Chinese chiming chisel entrenched	ostrich spinach vouch detach detachment	chinchilla cochineal mischievous surcharge handkerchief		ch
match ditch clutch scratch notch	sketch crutch stretch switch	hitch-hike ketchup hotch-potch catchment	slapstick hopscotch dispatch bewitch		tch
question digestion combustion	indigestion exhaustion suggestion congestion				ti
cello	cellist				c

t — Sound Group 31

top tart test tint tuft tot	tactful talent tasty tantrum textile	tentative testator tale-teller tantamount tripartite	inconsistent omnipotent incompetent impertinent entertainment		t
gate route kite mute crate mote	granite senate private minute devote	opposite composite infinite cultivate destitute	investigate substituted redistributed constituted instituting		te
button watt butt putt cattle kettle	tattoo lettuce cotton gutted twitter	permitted committee regretting forgotten boycotting			tt

intersect indict abstract victim verdict	You don't really hear the c, but you hear a pause, so put a letter.				ct
debt doubt	subtle debtor doubtless	subtlety "It's bad to be in de**b**t."			bt
receipt	You get one when you pay.				pt
yacht	yachting yachtsman I want to say ya-ch-t !	yachtsmanship			cht
cigarette gazette gavotte	cassette palette burette pipette	brunette omelette	flannelette serviette		tte
thyme	thymic	Thomas			th
veldt					dt
chopped	See Sound Group 39 p. 144, d at the end of words				ed

z — Sound Group 32

zoo zoom zone zero zinc zeal	quiz waltz fez whi quartz	zebra zephyr zither z zany crazy	breezy frenzy wizard lazy zeppelin	zinnia zodiac zealously zoology	z
prize craze size maize	trapeze capsize amaze	capsizable amazement sneezeweed	criticize minimize syllabize		ze

					ch
glaze	ablaze	breezeway	ostracize		
puzzle buzz jazz fizz muzzle	guzzled embezzle bedazzle razzle-dazzle	sizzling drizzly buzzard grizzly	frizziness grizzlier mezzanine embezzlement		zz
logs posy pansy spasm chasm	posies cosmos houses browses	residuals provisos fiascos dynamos	antagonism euphemism euthanasia microcosm		s
rose fuse rise vase these surprise	noise braise cause phrase ease	surmise chastise propose disused refused	diagnose Japanese analyse paraphrase hypotenuse		se
scissors	dessert dissolve	possession			ss
boy's toys					's
xylophone xyster xenolith	anxiety xylotomy	(auxiliary) xylonite	xenophobia,		x

Sound Group 33

zh

				s
measure treasure pleasure closure leisure erasure	enclosure disclosure composure exposure			s
television invasion evasion fusion lesion	provision collision confusion decision adhesion intrusion incision conclusion	occasion division corrosion revision precision persuasion illusion supervision		si

y   Sound Group 34

yacht yard yak youth year	yellow yodel youngest youthful				y
onion union junior million billion	pinion valiant brilliant stallion				i
Jugoslav		hallelujah			j

w   Sound Group 35

web well wet wind wag	wither winter waggon wallet	shadowy arrowroot yellowfish safflower	foreshadow disavow bungalow overthrow		w
quick quilt quack quest quite suite suave	quarterly quadrangle quality quadruped suede anguish dissuade	inquiry liquify inquisitive language persuade assuage suasion	consequently subsequent delinquent iniquitous sanguine languish		u
choir	boudoir memoir coiffure	reservoir			o
wh wheel when where whiff whip which	whine white while whale whirl	whimper whitening whisper whipping whatever	wheeze whisker whenever wharf		wh

Sound Group 36 — m

man mop mum mint mesh mate	member mimic moment mumbling memoir	remember immemorial dismember anemometer	memorandum momentum optimism pessimism minimum		m
hammer drummer swimming stammer summer hemming	mammal mammoth summon common gimmick	persimmon mideury.m., commandeer commiserate commission			mm
game grime fame tome fume	sublime presume inflame perfume	timely homestead sameness shameful	pantomime maritime metronome aerodrome		me
emblem	system problem anthem				em
lamb limb comb crumb climb	succumb benumb entomb coxcomb	honeycomb disentomb catacomb aplomb			mb
autumn hymn damn	condemn solemn column				
blossom bottom wisdom fathom venom custom	freedom kingdom symptom seldom				om
palm calm balm qualm	psalm salmon psalmist qualmish	becalm embalm			lm
program	(programme)				mme
phlegm	diaphragm epiphragm				gm

Jenny's Sound Dictionary

n   Sound Group 37

<u>nest</u>					n
nun	nineteenth	nonagon	nonconformist		
ninth	nonsense	banana	nonagenarian		
none	contend	dependent	nomination		
neon	canine	enhance	genuine	nonentity	
				frankincense	
<u>dinner</u>					nn
inn	manner	antennae	reconnaissance		
finn	thinner	forerunner	disconnection		
linn	sunning	biannual	innocently		
tonnage		perennial	annotation		
pennant		unannounced	annuitant		
<u>knife</u>					kn
knot	knapsack	knowledgeable			
knee	knowledge	knicker-bockers			
know	knighthood	acknowledging			
knight	knitting	unknowingly			
knoll	knocking				

> The **kn**owledgeable **kn**ight **kn**ows about **kn**aves and **kn**ackers who **kn**it **kn**ickerbockers and **kn**ock their **kn**obbly **kn**ees when **kn**eeling, begging to the cook **kn**eading dough with a **kn**ife and her **kn**uckles for bread to fill their **kn**apsacks before **kn**otting them.

<u>gnaw</u> (See Sound Group 37 p. 141 for gn at the end of words.)			gn
gnat	gnomic	gnashing	
gnash	gnosis	gnomon	
gnome	gnarled		
gnu	gnawing		
gnaw			

> The **gn**ome **gn**ashed his teeth at the **gn**at **gn**awing the **gn**u.

<u>pneumonia</u>	pneumatic		pn
<u>Wednesday</u>			dne
<u>grandpa</u>	sandwich	grandma	nd
<u>mnemonics</u>			mn
<u>epergne</u>	champagne	eau-de-Cologne	gne

Jenny's Sound Dictionary

n (near the end of words)

<u>engine</u> shone none pine one done	vaccine benzine cocaine sardine quinine	imagine examine determine discipline genuine	quarantine tangerine caffeine heroine		ne
<u>chicken</u> golden deafen sweeten frighten smarten	worsen freshen	enlighten citizen beholden forgotten dishearten	overburden shortening	moisten listen glisten fasten soften	en
<u>elephant</u>* thousand garland *See Sound Group 2, p. 98	brigand Shetland	England			an
<u>curtain</u> boatswain coxswain chaplain bargain	Britain captain certain villain	porcelain chamberlain mountainous			ain

I'm cert**ain** no capt**ain** needs a curt**ain** up a mount**ain**.
No capt**ain** wants to barg**ain** with a vill**ain** by a fount**ain**.

<u>lion</u> dragon ribbon tendon falcon siphon	common summon python mutton dungeon	religion imprison jettison beckoning abandon	comparison orpington		on
<u>basin</u> cousin satin	origin aspirin	muffin raisin			in
<u>sign</u> reign deign feign assign	consign resign ensign countersign	condign benign align			gn
<u>foreign</u>	sovereign				eign

Foreign: Why difficult? For Every Indian Girl's Name is foreign to most people from England.

Jenny's Sound Dictionary

ng Sound Group 38

sing cling wing sting spring	flinging swinging stringing bringing			ing
song gong strong long thong	belong furlong prolong oblong	songster thronging belongings diphthong	billabong	o ng
boomerang slang fang hang sprang	gangway gangster hanger mustang	boomerang coat hanger		a ng
rung flung swung hung lung	bunger stung			u ng
length lengthy strength	lengthen lengthwise strengthen			e ng
tongue harangue	tongue-tied meringue			ngue
finger angle mangle tingle bangle new-fangled	hanker singlet hunger monger	stronger mongrel Tongan thinker	linger angry hungry bungler	n

Jenny's Sound Dictionary

d (at the end of words) — Sound Group 39

spade					de
hide	explode	gratitude	barricade		
fade	stampede	marmalade	cavalcade		
strode	grenade	solitude	insecticide		
ride	provide	coincide	escalade		
add					dd
ladder	bedding	paddle			
daddy	ridden	budding			
peddle	coddle				
fiddle	nodding				
chopped					ed
fined	finished	rubbed			
stepped	jumped	inscribed	informed		
hopped	fished	absorbed	pronounced	governed	
filled	missed	advanced	experienced	rubbished	
tried	shocked	managed			
crowd					d
find	absurd	remind	found*		
scald	defend	expand	wound*		
word	record	resound	sold*		
herd	orchard	descend	told*		
heard*					
For words ending in ld, see Sound Group 11 p. 110 oul.					id

*Note: These words, though the action is finished, do not end in ed. They may be easily formed from the present tense in the following manner:

a. write the present tense: sell
b. say the past tense: sold
c. decide which sounds change...
d. change sell to sold

tell	told
find	found
hold	held
wind	wound
hear	heard
grind	ground

Jenny's Sound Dictionary

Sound Group 40

b

baby				b
bob	bamboo	barbaric		
bib	barber	barbecue		
bad	baboon	Biblical		
bend	bubble	bubonic		
but	bobbin	bilabial		
bubbles				bb
scrabble	dabbling	cobwebby		
squabble	bobbing	rubbished		
pebble	rubber	snobbishly		
nibble	rabbit	rubbery		
scribble	cabbage	shabbily		
globe				be

Sound Group 41

p

pig					p
pat	paper	populate	apart		
pop	piping	popular	aperture		
pup	poplin	Papuan	aptitude		
pip	puppy	propeller	apostrophe		
poop	poppy	propaganda	apology		
puppy					pp
scrappy	shopping	pepper	appal		
choppy	shipping	puppet	appeal		
snappy	wrapping	trapper	applaud		
poppy	ripping	supper	appliance		
happy	dripping	happen	appreciative		
grape					pe

Sound Group 42

h

hat		h
who?		wh
whom	wholly	
whole	wholesale	
whose	wholesome	
whoop	whooping	

Jenny's Sound Dictionary

(same letter, different sound)   **Letter-Based Groups**

Join the first two columns to make a word. Then add the 3rd column to make another word.

ough

	th	ough	t	b	ough	t
	th	ough		pl	ough	
	en	ough		br	ough	t
	thr	ough	t	r	ough	
	thor	ough		dr	ough	t
	thor	ough		tr	ough	
		ough	ly	b	ough	
				t	ough	
				d	ough	
				c	ough	
				s	ough	t
				f	ough	t
				over-wr	ough	t
				n	ough	t

a. I have thought about though, enough about though.
I ought to have thought enough about though.
So I shall look through these o-u-g-h words and learn them all thoroughly.

b. I bought a plough and brought it home. The track was rough because of a drought. My horse had a drink at a roadside trough.
I ate my lunch in the shade of a bough. The meat was tough and the bread was dough and it made me cough so I tossed it away. The dogs my lunch sought, and how they fought, and oh, how I was overwrought, and all for nought.

augh

dr	augh	t	
l	augh		
c	augh		
n	augh	ty	
h	augh	ly	
d	augh	ter	
t	augh	t	
sl	augh	ter	

A father was standing in a dr**augh**t, and he didn't l**augh** for he c**augh**t his n**augh**ty, h**augh**ty d**augh**ter and t**augh**t her not to sl**augh**ter.

our

	our	age has	c**our**age
on	our		hon**our**
in	our		fav**our**
	our	fav**our**ite	flav**our**
for	our		n**our**ishment
	our	eight	neighb**our**s
see	our		behavi**our**
hear	our		clam**our**
notice	our	ard**our** and	ferv**our**
Mother likes	our		col**our**s
	our		c**our**t
	our		c**our**tesy
	our	keys for the	j**our**ney
	our		demean**our**
	our		endeav**our**

Jenny's Sound Dictionary

X — Letter-Based Groups

x = /ks/ coax excuse expand exquisite next exclaim explain experience Saxon sixty exchange explicit saxophone ox execute extricate dexterity	x
x = /gz/ exist exalt exemplary examination exam example exaggerate exasperate	x
x = /gz/ (luxury) luxuriant	x
x = /kz/ luxury anxious inflexion noxious	x
x = k except exception excite excellent excel	x
x = ks axe	xe
x = z anxiety	x
xi = sh anxious	xi

Irregular Words

colonel
tongue
meringue
rhyme
suite
choir
sure
quay

One day the queen went to the quay.

Appendices

Appendix 1 Writing Revision

This section is to be used at the teacher's discretion, if a student is uncertain or confused as to the formation of letters. There will be lots of writing during the course, and the student needs to be able to concentrate on the making of words. The hints in this section follow the order of letters on the Writing Chart, a copy of which may be laminated and given to the student if this is desirable.

Figure 13: The Writing Chart

Row 1	i	t	h	b	th
Row 2	r	n	m	p	k
Row 3	c	d	g	j	ch
Row 4	v	y	w	qu	wh
Row 5	z	x	s	f	sh
Row 6	i	u	o	a	e

Writing Revision: Beginning

See that student has pen and lined writing paper, and introduce the Writing Chart (Figure 13, previous page).

To write we have to think, so we need to use our brains, ears, fingers, eyes and hands. What do our hands do? One holds our pencil and writes but what does the other do? It helps by indicating the left-to right direction that the writing must take. For a right-hander, the left hand says to the writing hand, "Go that way." Insert arrow → (For a left-hander, the right hand says, "Come this way.") Insert arrow → so that we always know which way our writing should go.

Now how do we start? With the 1st row on the chart.

Writing the Consonants

ROW 1

The first row of letters – i, t, h, b, th – all utilise the same basic down stroke formation. DRAW five lines, one in each box, for each different letter.

l for lamp – start above the line and go down to touch the line. It stands tall and straight like a lamp post.

t for tent – tall, straight line going down to the ground with a cross in the middle for the roof support.

h for hat on the chair – (the letter looks like a chair). A tall straight back rest then up and across for the cushion and back down to the floor.

b for greedy boy eating apples – (let's follow where the apples go) straight down his throat and into his tummy, up and over and down then back to where his tummy started.

th for three of us saying thanks for our chair – th makes a double sound, so we need to write two letters. First t then h.

ROW 2

The next row of letters – r, n, m, p, k – also utilise the same basic down stroke movement, thus giving students a continued common base from which to start and succeed.

r for running rabbit – (he stands and hops). A little line down then up and over and stop. Remember he is only small and his hop is not too long, not too short, just right.

n for nest – (let's cover the eggs so they don't get cold). They are only little eggs, so we start with a small line down then we go up and over and straight back down again.

m for mouse – start with a small stroke down, up and over and down (to make his body) then up and over and down again (to make his head).

p for pig – start with a small stroke going down, but make it go past our line and down (because the pig's feet have sunk into the mud). Now go back up his feet to the top of the mud and let's make his head: up and over and down, then back to where his head started.

k for kitten – tall stroke down then up and over (like h, but he swings in and out and back to the ground), then back to touch the down stroke and kick his leg out and touch the line.

ROW 3

The next row of letters – c, d, g, j, ch – utilise either the basic anti-clockwise ellipse or a down stroke or a combination of these two movements. However, they all employ some movement to the left first (all others have gone right as the first sideways direction).

c for cat – let's 'make the cat curl up into a ball'. Start above the ground line, go left and down, curl up again when you touch the line, but don't go right back to the start.

d for dog – it's just like a c only we join it up and add a tail. Start above the line, go left and down, curl up at the line and touch where you started, keep going up (tail in the air) then back down the same stroke and finish on the line.

g for girl with long hair – (just like a d but instead of a tail, she has long hair she can sit on). Start above the line, go left and down, curl up at the line and touch where you started; now go down past the line (for her hair) and finish with curl to the left (so she can sit on her hair).

j for jug – let's make the handle for the jug (just like a **g**) without the girl's head). Start above the line, go down past it and finish with a curl to the left (so the handle joins onto the jug). Lift your pencil and put a dot above where you started because we splashed some milk picking up the jug.

ch for church where we sit on a chair – ch makes a double sound, so we need to write two letters. Firstly c then h.

ROW 4

The next row of letters – v, y, w, qu, wh – utilises the basic downstroke and flick up.

v for van – start above the line, go down to the line then quickly turn and flick up and to the right.

y for yacht – this starts like v, down to the line then turn the corner and flick up and to the right. Then straight down below the line and curl to the left (remember to go under the water to put the keel).

w for web (looks like we put v and v together). Start above the line, go down and touch the line then turn and flick up and to the right, repeat the whole thing. Down to the line then turn the corner and flick up and to the right.

qu for queen – q needs its helper u to make a sound, so we need to write two letters. Firstly q. Start above the line, go left and down, curl up at the line and touch where you started, now go down past the line (for her train) and finish with a flick right (so her page can hold her train). Then u – (it has to hold lots of things, so it is open at the top), down the line then turn the corner and flick up and to the right, then go straight back down to finish on the line.

wh for whistle and "I will have to whistle for a chair" – wh makes a double sound, so we will have to write two letters. Firstly w then h.

ROW 5

The next row of letters – z, x, s, f, sh – utilise a mixture of straight and curved lines.

z for zebra – (follow the zebra's directions to the zoo). Start above the line and go straight to the right, stop, change, and go crosswise down and back to the left, stop at the line and go back to the right along the line.

x as in box – let's make a cross inside a box. We will have to go from the corners of the box only. Start at the top left corner and go crosswise down to the right. Now pick up your pencil and start with the other top corner (top right), this time we have to go back to the bottom left corner crossing the first stroke.

s for snake – (can you find the little c chasing the snake?) Start above the line and move left, then curl down and round and head back to the right, change direction (dodge the snake) curl down and to the left and finish.

f for fish with a long waving tail – start above the line, hook up then over to the left then straight down to the line. Don't forget to cross in the middle like f.

sh for snake-skin shoe – (a shoe is like a chair for your foot). sh makes a double sound, so we need to write two letters. Firstly s then h.

Writing the Vowels

ROW 6

We suggest the following order – i, u, o, a, e – for learning to write the vowels, as they proceed from the easiest to the hardest to produce in writing.

i for Indian – start above the line and make a short stroke down to it. Lift your pencil and put a dot above where you started to be his feather waving in the wind.

u for umbrella – to keep the rain off and it is the shape of the handle we hold. Down to the line then turn the corner and flick up and to the right, then go straight back down to finish on the line.

o for orange – (just like c but go back to the beginning and join up our lines). Start above the line, go left and down, curl up at the line and back to touch/finish where you started.

a for apple – (just like a c only we join it up and add the stalk that joins it to the tree). Start above the line, go left and down, curl up at the line, go back and touch where you started, then straight down and finish on the line.

e for egg – start above the line, 'cut the egg' first, stretch up and towards the right, curl back to the left then down past where we started and touch the line and curl to the right and up, but only go a little way and stop.

Appendix 2 Using the Recorder in Remedial Tutoring

Using a recorder in remedial/catch-up sessions helps to vary the teaching, and provides essential reinforcement of learning.

Because of this, it is possible to minimise the number and frequency of the sessions required if the recorder is properly used.

During each session activity, the student records significant teaching sequences, as indicated by the teacher. This helps to focus the student's attention, and also occupies their hands when they are not writing.

The student learns to take directions from the recording. This helps their ability to listen and respond appropriately.

It also allows for repetition of instructions if this is necessary.

Between sessions, the student reviews the recording and does additional tasks indicated on the recording by the teacher. This increases the student's confidence in their ability to work independently, since no adult needs to be present.

Using the recording helps students with visual perception difficulties because they can build on their auditory strength. It can help students with auditory processing weakness to develop in that area.

There are two kinds of recordings:

"X"- recordings are "explain" recordings which review the session activity just completed. They contain explanations of the work by teacher and student.

"Z"- recordings are Zoom recordings. These are for revision. There is an emphasis on completing them quickly: hence their name. However, students respond much better to the name "Z"– recording than to "Revision Recording".

Appendix 3 Adaptations for Whole Class Work

It seems a shame that some educators wait until students have had the devastating experience of failure at school, associated with spelling and reading, before a concerted effort is undertaken to rectify the problem. Although this program was originally designed with remediation in mind, it actually lends itself to successful use with a whole class setting by helping to eliminate negative attitudes towards the skills of 'encoding' and 'decoding' through its challenging presentation. Thus spelling becomes fun and successful, a rare recurrence for a majority of both children and adults.

We are teaching the student listening and reasoning skills rather than focusing on visual memory or the alphabet approach, neither of which seems to be have been totally successful with all students. We encourage students to become active, not passive listeners, and to think logically and sequentially, which are useful skills in other areas of school work. We are dealing with the association of ideas that go hand in hand with phonic grouping of letters within words. Students are trained to link new sounds to words to previous experiences and when they become familiar with the way letters go together, become very creative and adept at finding their associations, which of course have more impact because they are personal and peculiar to each student.

The following ideas constitute the easiest means of modifying the program for use within the classroom, or indeed for all small schools, with the whole school.

An overhead data projector can be used in conjunction with enlarged and reduced copies to create highly visible pages for varying size groups. Initial treatment of each reference page can be effectively done with the projector – then students break into smaller groups to complete follow-up tasks adjusted to individual needs and abilities.

A recording device and listening post is an excellent means for individualising work, effectively allowing the teacher to be in more than one place at a time, with a group in person and with multiple groups on the recording. Reference pages can be reviewed; extra word groups practised and individualised; and discovery learning stressed.

The making of class-sized-posters of reference pages to be used as visually accessible reminders around the room, is another effective teaching tool. They also allow students to share work discoveries with classmates without the threat involved in sharing their own personal reference copies. These large pages can then be turned into a class/school ' reference book' for everyone to use.

Drama is a fabulous, enjoyable way to introduce support 'clues' found within the program. All the situations are ones that the children have personal experience with – animal mothers and babies (cats and kittens): traffic signs and their effects on drivers; friends and how they help each other; safe and dangerous situations, how to recognise them and what we can do when confronted with them.

This scaffold approach to new words and lists of words demands the students' full attention, draws on all their creative talents and entails participation that challenges the student with clues and links. This should be the way students find words and spend time on words.

DON'T TRY TO LEARN WORDS – DISCOVER THEM

Appendix 4 Additional Words for Seniors

a. Talk To Pencil – 'Safe' Words

us	unit	eleven	athletic	unexpected
van	edit	editor	optimist	isolated
tap	oval	animal	ignorant	elevated
fan	over	banana heroic	mandolin	diagonal
nap	solid	panama	romantic	panorama
bad	under	safari	repented	diameter
dab	music	sahara	provided	continental
man	relax	apricot	disposal	violinist
vet	until	rotunda	momentum	escalator
hen	equip	visitor	rotating	binocular
set	paper	gradual	tolerant	indicated
win	adult	popular	enrolment	parabolic
nip	elect	elegant	replenish	aluminium
din	model	develop	equipment	experiment
not	bacon	acrobat	sensitive	competitor
pin	artist	musical	expensive	impediment
mop	lumber	omnibus	september	propaganda
tot	wizard	parapet	exchanged	optimistic
hop	depend	inhabit	president	pessimistic
cog	report	cabinet	unselfish	memorandum
nod	induct	caravan	indignant	arithmetic
pop	melted	stadium	disputed	pedestrian
rod	sunday	rivulet	permanent	locomotive
tub	friday	evident	contented	development
rug	moment	invented	establish	impertinent
bun	select	calendar	confident	independent
rut	linger	penitent	persisted	temperament
fun	victim	relative	conductor	thermometer
mud	rumpus	sediment	represent	significant
bus	legend	terminus	impulsive	comparative
bud	propel	organist	interpret	extravagant
nut	within	together	reflected	antibiotic
tug	porter	domestic	perfected	dilapidated
set	hectic	mandarin	predicted	redecorated
top	compel	vertical	disregard	cosmopolitan
plan	vacant	consider	dramatist	hippopotamus
flap	darwin	canister	enchanted	agricultural
dent	danish	abundant	departing	incorporated
mend	demand	monastic	herbalist	redevelopment
tent	vanish	critical	extensive	transcontinent
trip	secret	majestic	important	representative
brig	selfish		archbishop	

pith	tempted	romantic	consistent
brim	depend	hospital	dependable
slid	darling	cardigan	membership
dish	refresh	motorist	department
frog	reflect	dominant	understand
pump	carting	remember	instructed
thud	costing	disorder	thermostat
plug	conduct	personal	protesting
this	respect	astonish	punishment
that	publish	dramatic	clambering
then	shining	artistic	preventing
them	sprinted	insisted	persisting
scrap	misprint	intended	compliment
strap	standing	interest	constructed

With Seniors these words are a winner!

b. Talk To Pencil – 'Danger' Words

use	oxide	avenue	devaluate
mate	value	educate	elaborate
mane	unite	operate	apologise
tame	amuse	realise	humiliate
tape	fortune	penalise	habituate
save	tadpole	navigate	retaliate
fame	consume	diagnose	inviolate
safe	dilute	estimate	evaporate
win	dispute	latitude	deliberate
pipe	nature	graduate	amalgamate
nine	behave	excavate	co-ordinate
mile	repose	separate	invigorate
tide	severe	organise	obliterate
dine	estate	emigrate	manipulate
ride	volume	abdicate	repopulate
dive	admire	parasite	depopulate
time	secure	hesitate	devitalise
note	senate	absolute	dilapidate
mole	impose	envelope	deactivate
pope	advise	decorate	substitute
home	refuse	advocate	obliterate
hope	endure	continue	continuate
cone	manure	saturate	impregnate
rope	escape	indicate	dehumanize
bone	repute	inundate	electorate
rode	invite	moderate	perpetuate
vote	rescue	aptitude	revitalise
tube	depose	antidote	ingratitude
fuse	arcade	liberate	impersonate
tune	explode	hibernate	unfortunate
dune	private	departure	investigate
muse	promote	obstinate	agriculture
mute	brigade	gratitude	temperature
cute	enclose	persevere	discontinue
cube	pasture	advertise	domesticate
plane	futile	vestibule	
	underexpose		
state	pantomime	intemperate	
		deteriorate	
	interfere	manufacture	
	candidate	considerate	
	improvise	incriminate	
	metronome	reconstitute	
	chocolate	discriminate	
	adventure		

explore

fertilize
recognize
cultivate

migrate
complete
membrane
sunshine
campfire
inscribe
describe

costume
shade
bathe
flame
waste
blame
tripe
shine

prone
stone
paste
clothe

enclosure
pasture
indoctrinate
terminate
inarticulate
overestimate
demilitarize
multitude
arbitrate
crocodile
cavalcade
temperate
misfortune
complicate

propose
capsule
confuse
cascade
athlete
capture

trapeze
provide
venture
extreme
scope

slide
value
argue
stone

conglomerate
tantalize
bride
smile
chime
slope
disorientate
intermediate
undergraduate
underestimate
insubordinate
inconsiderate
indiscriminate
congratulate

Appendix 5 Illustrations for Processing Words

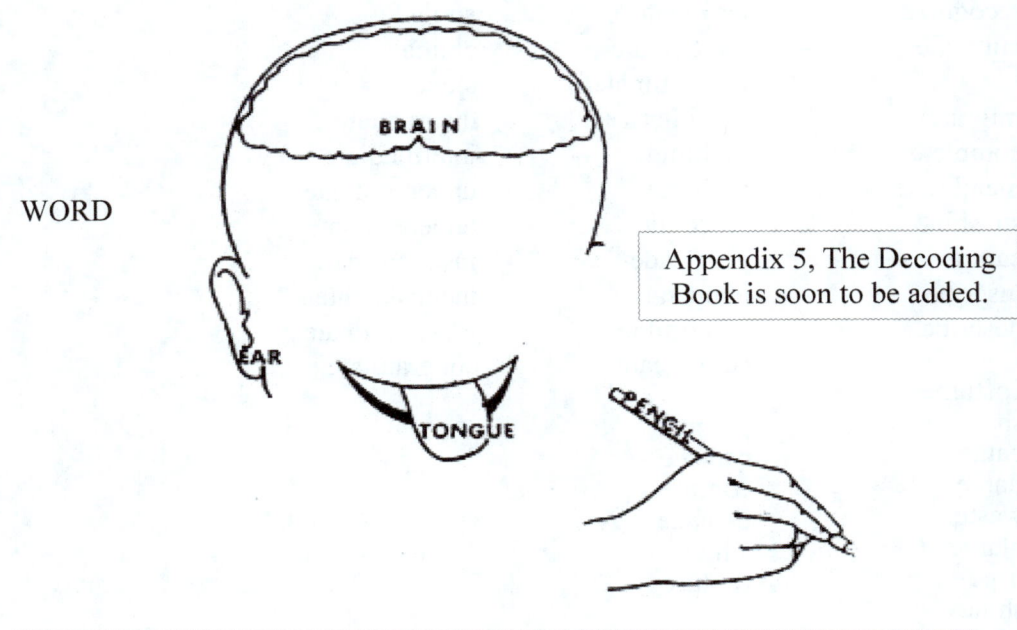

WORD

Appendix 5, The Decoding Book is soon to be added.

Which way does the WORD travel? THINK and CHOOSE.
Draw in the WORD travelling to your Pencil.

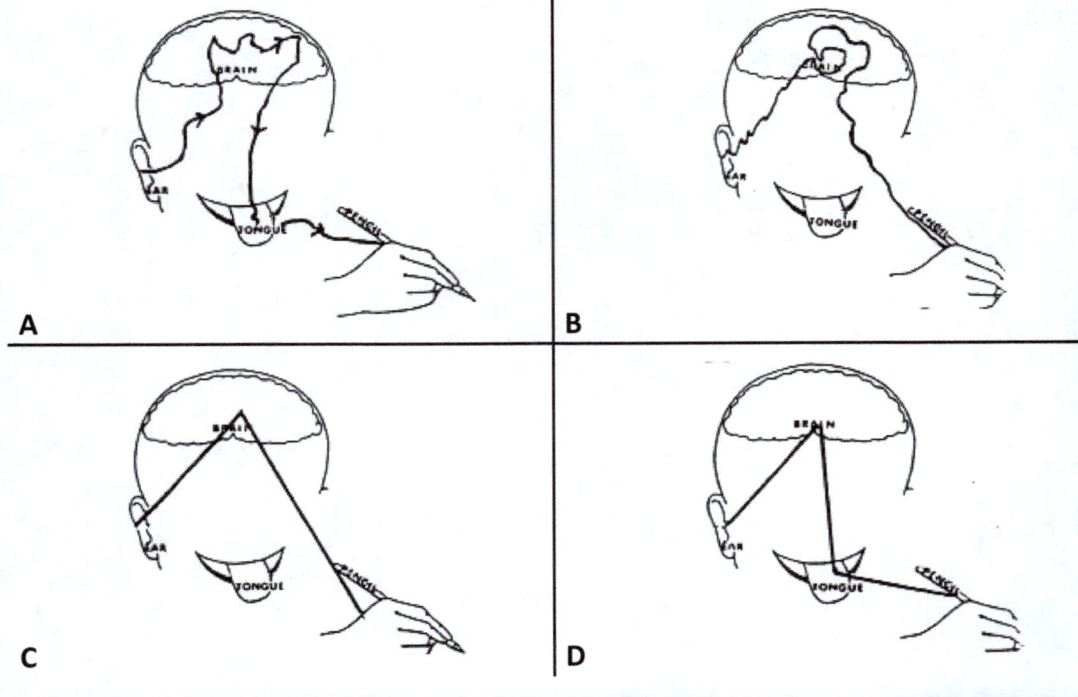

A B C D

162   Appendices

Appendices 163

Appendix 6 Activity Plan and Activity Templates

ACTIVITY PLAN
Discovering Reading and Spelling through Sound

ACTIVITY	1	2	3	4	5	6	7
SOUND CHARTS	The beginning SOUND	Consonants & Vowels	Revision – Make your own vowel charts	Both charts displayed for reference			
Discovering Rd & Sp Through Sounds TUTORS Handbook [Page REFERENCES for each Activity]			Listening 1 sound, 2 sounds	Talk to Pencil	Danger Vowels & Bossy 'e'	'e' or 'I'	Double Letters
RECORDING		For each individual – record activity dialog for later revision. Add additional words for later individual work.					
SPELLING LISTS			Make your own writing chart	Words from school lists can be spelt using the rules so far taught, or using "talk-to-the-pencil" principle.			
DECODING BOOK [Student activity]				Begin your own Start to 'put away' important words and do a little word building.			
READING	Provide support and reassurance as auditory skills grow, sound/word connections start to make sense and words are spoken with accurate sound pronunciation.						
JENNY'S SOUND DICTIONARY	The Student begins to build up word families according to their sounds.						

8	9	10	11	12	13	14	15	16	17
Also make Safe & Danger Vowel Chart available for reference									
'c' & 'k'	'c' & 'k' to finish	'k' only 1 friend	'c' only 1 friend	When 'g' says 'jjj'					
Record activities plus additional words.					Make "x-plan" recordings based on spelling lists. Periodic "Z-oom" recordings for revision.				
					Begin "detective pages". Intensive work on word families based on words from weekly spelling lists.				
					Begin oral reading. Analyse problems (see page 60). Teach how to use the "PUSHER" for fluency (see page 129).				

Appendices 165

Activity 2.0 - Consonant Picture Chart

c	d	g	j	ch
s	r	n	m	sh
l	t	h	b	th
f	k	p	x	qu
v	y	w	z	wh

Appendices

Consonant Letter Chart

c	d	g	j	ch
s	r	n	m	sh
l	t	h	b	th
f	k	p	x	qu
v	y	w	z	wh

Consonant Word Chart

cat	dog	girl	jug	church
snake	rabbit	nest	mouse	shoe
lamp	tent	hat	boy	three
fish	kitten	pig	box	queen
van	yacht	web	zebra	whistle

Activity 2. Extension work – Blank Chart

___	___	___	___	___
___	___	___	___	___
___	___	___	___	___
___	___	___	___	___
___	___	___	___	___

Activity 3
LISTENING – ONE sound, TWO sounds?

Activity 4.
SAFE and DANGER vowel Chart

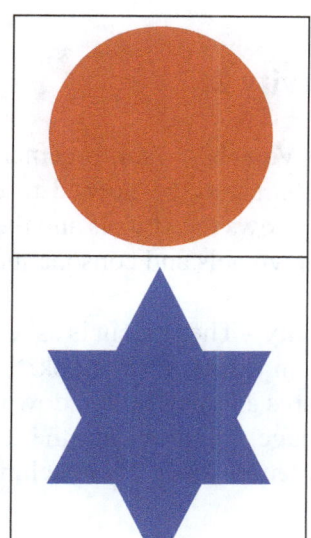

Fig. 12

EXTENTION ACTIVITY TEMPLATES

These templates can be copied for a student to use to make his/her own vowel chart.

Activity 2

Safe Vowels – Reinforcement of skill with the chart may be needed to ensure the student knows the vowels and the difference between vowels and consonants.

Activity – The student is asked to go to a new page in their activity book. Then cut out the pictures and paste them down the left side of the page. Then cut out the letters and paste each letter beside the matching picture.

Activity 5

Safe and Danger Vowels – Reinforcement of the skill with the chart may be needed to ensure the student has a firm grasp of the concept and can differentiate between the short sound 'safe' vowel sounds and the long 'danger' vowel sounds.

Activity – The student is asked to go to a new page in their activity book, rule a line down the middle. One the left side with green pencil write the word 'SAFE' and in the right column with a red pencil write the word 'DANGER'. Then cut out the pictures and letters and paste each letter beside the matching picture in the Green 'safe' vowel column or the Red 'danger'.

Activity 5.
Teachers Page

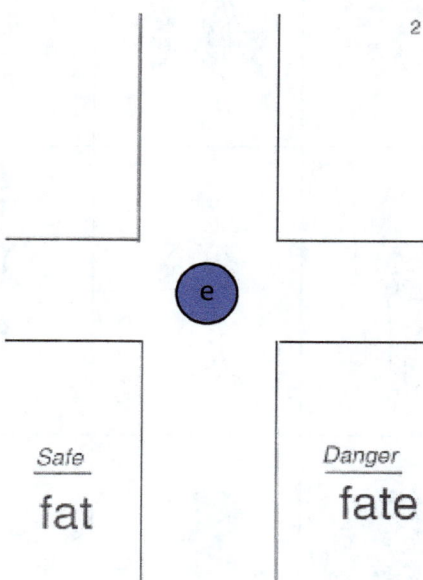

Appendices 171

Activity 6 Student's Page 5				
Activity 7 Student's Page 7				
Activity 8 Student's Page 9				
Activity 8.b Student's Page 11.a				
Activity 8.b Cont… Student's Page 11.b				

Activity 9 Student's Page 13				
Activity 10 Student's Page 15				
Activity 11 Student's Page 17			Activity 11 Page 19	
Activity 12 Student's Page 21				

Index

A
Accent 94
Auditory 5, 7, 11, 14, 17, 26, 30, 32, 36, 39, 89–90, 155, 164

B
Bossy–e 14, 43, 45, 47, 60–61, 76–77
Bossy–i 45, 47, 60–61
Bossy–y 45, 47, 60–61

C
Catchy 71–74, 84, 87, 91
Clues 10, 17, 40, 42, 50, 66, 71, 73–74, 77, 83–84, 86–87, 89, 94, 97, 157
Consonants 14, 16, 20, 23, 151, 164, 170

D
Danger 14–15, 17, 32–34, 39–41, 49, 51, 73, 81–83, 160, 164–165, 169–170
Decoding 4–5, 7, 10, 12, 14, 17–18, 25–26, 28, 30–31, 32, 36, 39–40, 43, 47, 49–50, 53, 56, 60, 62, 82–84, 156, 164
Detective 2, 15, 57, 71, 83, 88–91, 133, 165
Dictionary 5, 14, 16–17, 26, 57, 71, 79, 81–83, 87, 89, 93–94, 97, 164
Discovery 16–19, 62, 102, 156

E
Eye 11, 64–67, 69, 105
Eyetracking 9

H
Handwriting 5, 17
Hear 2, 6, 8, 16, 27–28, 30–31, 36, 43, 60, 65, 76–77, 89–90, 95, 114, 137, 144, 146

K
Kinders 16

L
Letter 5, 7, 10, 13, 16–28, 32–33, 37, 43–44, 47, 49, 53–54, 56, 60, 67, 69, 73–76, 81–83, 89–90, 92, 95, 106, 108, 113–114, 118, 122–123, 127, 129, 135, 137, 146–147, 151, 167, 170
Letters 3, 8, 11, 14, 16–21, 23, 27–28, 30, 36, 39, 43–44, 47, 53, 55–56, 60, 74, 78, 81–85, 87, 89–91, 150–154, 156, 164, 170
Listen 3, 16, 19, 26–27, 36, 53, 60, 65, 76–77, 82–83, 86–87, 126, 142, 155
Listening 3, 5, 14, 16, 18, 26–28, 38, 87, 156, 164, 169

M
Mnemonic 16, 73, 82, 89, 106

O
Orthography 73
Outcomes 5

P
Phonics 7, 9, 132
Pre–schoolers 16
Processing 2, 6–7, 11–12, 155, 162

R
Read 2, 6–7, 9–12, 17–18, 20, 30, 36, 49, 53, 58, 60, 62, 65–71, 100
Remedial 2–4, 7, 64, 67, 83, 89–90, 96, 155

S

Safe 15, 17, 23–24, 30, 32–35, 39, 49, 62, 73, 81–83, 131, 157–158, 160, 165, 169–170
Safety 23, 40–41, 51
Scaffold 157
Scaffolded 86
Sight words 17
Sound 2, 5–7, 11, 13–14, 16–20, 23–30, 33–34, 36, 38, 43, 47, 49, 51, 53, 55–58, 60, 66, 71, 73, 79, 81–85, 89, 91–134, 136–141, 143–146, 151, 153–154, 164, 169–170
Sounds 1, 3, 5–7, 14, 16–20, 23–28, 30, 36–37, 47, 53, 56, 66, 71, 73, 77, 81–85, 87–88, 91, 94, 96, 144, 164, 169–170
Spell 3, 18, 28
Spelling 1–6, 9, 14–15, 19, 23, 28, 46, 50, 62, 64, 69, 72–73, 82–84, 86, 88–89, 92, 94, 96, 109, 111, 114, 156, 164–165
Student 2–6, 8, 12, 14, 16–20, 23–26, 30, 32–34, 36, 38–39, 42–43, 47, 49, 52–53, 56, 58, 60, 62–64, 71, 78, 83–84, 150–151, 155–157, 164, 170
Syllables 30, 48–49, 51–52, 71, 87
Symbol 6–7, 16, 20, 95, 104, 131
Symbols 6, 8, 17, 95

T

Talk to the pencil 2
Tutor 30, 46–47

V

Vocabulary 74
Vowels 14, 16–17, 20, 23, 32, 82, 93, 154, 164, 170

W

Word 2–3, 5, 8–11, 14–17, 19, 22, 26–31, 33, 36–39, 47–49, 53–54, 56, 65–67, 69–78, 82–87, 89–91, 93–94, 123, 129, 144, 146, 156, 162, 164–165, 167, 170
Words 2–3, 5, 8–12, 14–20, 23–26, 28, 30–31, 32–34, 36–41, 43–44, 46–51, 53–54, 56, 58–78, 81–84, 86–87, 89–90, 92, 94, 97–98, 109, 111, 114, 118, 122, 129, 137, 141–142, 144, 146–147, 150, 156–160, 162, 164–165
Write 2–3, 5, 10–11, 16–17, 23–24, 26–28, 30–31, 33, 36–37, 39, 43–44, 47, 49, 53–54, 56, 60, 62, 73–77, 83–84, 87, 91, 115, 144, 151, 153–154, 170
Writing 2–3, 6, 14, 16–18, 23, 30, 36–37, 41, 47, 54, 69, 89–90, 150–151, 154–155, 164

The Jenny Lamond Method

If you would like to know how to become
an accredited tutor of the **Jenny Lamond Method,**
please contact **Pat Grayson** of
Heartspace Publications, and of the
Jenny Lamond Literacy Foundation on:
pat@heartspacepublications.com
or call
+61 450260348
for information.

www.ingramcontent.com/pod-product-compliance
Lightning Source LLC
Chambersburg PA
CBHW060459010526
44118CB00018B/2468